WHAT IF . . .

Also by Shirley MacLaine

You Can Get There from Here

Don't Fall off the Mountain

Dancing in the Light

Out on a Limb

It's All in the Playing

Going Within

Dance While You Can

My Lucky Stars

The Camino

Out on a Leash

Sage-ing While Age-ing

I'm Over All That

WHAT IF . . .

A Lifetime of Questions,
Speculations, Reasonable Guesses,
and a Few Things I Know for Sure

SHIRLEY MACLAINE

ATRIA PAPERBACK
New York   London   Toronto   Sydney   New Delhi

ATRIA PAPERBACK

A Division of Simon & Schuster, Inc.
1230 Avenue of the Americas
New York, NY 10020

First Atria Paperback edition March 2014

ATRIA PAPERBACK and colophon are trademarks of Simon & Schuster, Inc.
Illustration on page viii: Joe Heller, © by *Green Bay Press–Gazette*.

For information about special discounts for bulk purchases, please contact Simon & Schuster Special Sales at 1-866-506-1949 or business@simonandschuster.com.

The Simon & Schuster Speakers Bureau can bring authors to your live event. For more information or to book an event, contact the Simon & Schuster Speakers Bureau at 1-866-248-3049 or visit our website at www.simonspeakers.com.

Designed by Jill Putorti
Jacket design by Janet Perr
Jacket photograph by Blake Little/Getty Images

Manufactured in the United States of America

10 9 8 7 6 5 4 3 2 1

Library of Congress Cataloging-in-Publication Data

MacLaine, Shirley, date.
    What if . . . : a lifetime of questions, speculations, reasonable guesses, and a few things I know for sure / Shirley MacLaine
        pages cm
1. MacLaine, Shirley, date. 2. Entertainers—United States—Biography. I. Title.
    PN2287.M18A3 2013
    791.4302'8092—dc23
    [B]   2013023970

ISBN 978-1-4767-2860-5
ISBN 978-1-4767-2861-2 (pbk)
ISBN 978-1-4767-2862-9 (ebook)

To Terry and Buddy-Bub

"All truth passes through three stages: First, it is ridiculed; second, it is violently opposed; third, it is accepted as self-evident."

—Arthur Schopenhauer

INTRODUCTION

It's Good Friday 2013, and I'm wondering what's so "good" about it. It seems that everywhere I go things are falling apart or a mess: wind and rain are turning into superstorms; road rage is an epidemic, maniacs behind the wheel even here in Santa Fe; shootings on freeways in L.A.; emotional terrorism from people in positions of authority in airports. On a daily basis packages are lost, products are defective, repairs never work, workmen don't show up, computers crash, the cable goes out. Asteroids and meteors fall to Earth, and governments are too paralyzed to help their people or themselves. Everyone talks about money all the time and where to get "a deal." People answer questions with more questions. New Yorkers plow ahead down the sidewalks or in the streets, not blinking at crippling traffic or noticing the ear-shattering noise of seemingly endless construction. Angelinos build their fences higher and bury their heads deeper. Nobody seems to talk with clarity. I just want to stay at home either in Malibu or Santa Fe. What is happening? Is this daily trauma of a thousand small pecks a wake-up call telling us that we, the human race, may simply have gone too far for a cleanup?

It's actually become a bad comedy to me: nothing works. Our once-disciplined work ethic has evaporated, and many people seem to be just waiting for time off so they can indulge in another handful of painkillers. People complain about unemployment, but for the most part, they don't like what they do anyway.

Thank goodness that's not my story. In my line of work, I've gotten to be a whole host of other people and I've gotten paid pretty well for it. But the truth is I'm not unique. All of us are really a collection of assorted people. Each of us is a myriad of personalities and identities; most of us simply have not caught up to the richness and complexity of who we really are. I am beginning to believe we are our own best entertainment. To paraphrase that wise man named Shakespeare, we are simply actors in our own self-created plays, believing that the fiction that we fancy is real.

Working in Hollywood, I live in a "what if" world, where there are multiple blue-sky meetings before any project: "What if the leading man is ugly instead of handsome?" "What if he doesn't die in the end?" "What if we think he's dead, but he's not?" Over the years, I've noticed that all these what-ifs in my "reel" life have led me to adopt a similarly speculative stance in my "real" life. There's a lot to be gained from asking yourself, "What if . . ."

For example, what if, on this Good Friday a couple of thousand years ago, Jesus didn't die on the Cross, but instead got married, had children, and traveled incognito for the rest of his life? What if Mary Magdalene was the missing mistress in the Last Supper paintings? What kind of impact would that have on the modern-day Church, its teachings, its sense of itself? There have been books bragging about various authors' research into such matters, and I'll admit I have read most of them, but not many exploring what such a fact would mean. I subscribe to the saying "One man's sacrilege is another man's truth." I like to think that I'm open to exploring *anything,* always questioning, trying to live free of preconceptions and blind certainties.

It's fun to speculate—it's an entertainment, and entertainment is my life. I've always believed that I owe my talent to my innate curiosity more than anything else. To me, imagination is more sacred and powerful than knowledge. Maybe we have even imagined ourselves into believing we are real when in fact we are a grand illusion dreamed up by some other species. Perhaps Shakespeare was right after all—and I mean literally correct, not metaphorically—when he wrote, "All the world's a stage, / And all the men and women merely players; / They have their exits and their entrances, [births and deaths] / And one man in his time plays many parts [has many identities] . . ." I know several intelligent scientists who believe it might be possible to prove that the human race and our dramatic shenanigans are actually an extraterrestrial pageant of some kind, with actors (that would be us!) who believe wholeheartedly in their characters' dramatic story arc—a "reality television" of sorts for the ETs.

That may be true, but I'm mindful of Stephen Hawking's warning: "Be careful of embracing extraterrestrial life, should there be such a thing. Remember what happened to the natives in North America with the arrival of the white man." That was a pretty bad "scene," wouldn't you say?

Stephen himself is a wonderful example of sophisticated, yet practical, illusion. It seems that he is confined to his wheelchair, incapable of moving anything but his right eye. But I believe he travels and moves about with more brilliance and curiosity than any other living person. I believe he leaves his body and soars in exploration of the cosmos, returning with reports of black holes and otherworldly civilizations.

I know him because for a time we had the same publisher. We met at parties and formed a friendship. When he'd come to America, I'd host parties for him, inviting people who weren't exactly part of my usual crowd, but I loved meeting them.

He has two pictures over his desk at Cambridge University: one of Marilyn Monroe and one of Albert Einstein. He told me (through his electronic chair) that "the curves of the universe are as beautiful as Miss Monroe." He also told me, and he has said so publicly, that he is certain he is the reincarnation of Sir Isaac Newton. He was born exactly three hundred years after Sir Isaac died, and he holds the Newton Chair at Cambridge.

Stephen Hawking is both a grand and a simple man. His intellect is without bounds, but it's his humor and wit that attract me. When he was more agile, I used to watch him gleefully maneuver his "golden" wheelchair around the streets of Cambridge, defying anyone to get in his way. The word spread quickly around the campus that Stephen was on the loose again—*Be alert!*

When I was in the United Kingdom shooting *Downton Abbey* in 2012, I emailed him, and he invited me to lunch, but I received the invitation a day late. I was crestfallen. It made me ask myself whether the speed of a loving thought was faster than the speed of light (186,282.397 miles a second) and if I had missed his invitation because of it. I called him and, through his caretaker, asked him the question. He took a while before he answered via his chair. "The two are not comparable," he said, making me laugh by giving such a scientific answer to my more "philosophical" question.

Maybe the truth is that *nothing* is comparable to anything else, particularly if each of us is our own universe and we create *everything* around us. That probably sounds like New Age blather, I know. But what if it's true? I sit and talk with other people, confident in my belief that they are actually there, but what if they are only in my creative daytime dream, just as they might sometimes turn up in my dreams at night? Even more important—what if my night dreams are the expression of my internal yin (female) side, and the daytime dream reality is an expression of my more demonstrative external yang (male) side? What if each of us needs to respect the night and day illusions equally?

I would have to say the daytime (yang) masculine expression of "reality" is what has reduced the human race to the deterioration we are now experiencing, whereas the nighttime (yin) female reality might have afforded us the opportunity to search with more compassion and keener accuracy for who we are and what we really want. Of one thing I am certain: I create everyone *and* their behavior in my dreams at night. Why is it so hard to admit we are creating the same thing during the turmoil of our busy days?

Stephen Hawking has made a career out of studying and reveling in his imaginative journey of the cosmos, using his curiosity as a means to overcome the "seeming reality" of his wheelchair-bound days. I am pleased that such a proof-driven scientist helps me to make my point about self-created illusion. Stephen is devoid of self-pity and *knows* he is grander than he might seem. He once said to me, "Those who think I don't believe in God don't know me." He looked up as if to show me he was seeing the "all there is," and I could imagine him thinking, "It's much more awe-inspiring than our human definitions of God." I thought to myself, "What if he sees so much more than any other human being because he isn't terribly concerned with his physical condition?" Is that the message of his living so long without earthbound priorities?

Did he "create" the disease that has crippled him in order to learn to be dependent on caregivers and the kindness of strangers so that he could free his entire mind to the pursuit of knowledge? What if he inadvertently chose to set an example of himself to show the rest of us that cosmic travel and universal understanding are available, regardless of one's physical condition or circumstance? If Jesus *chose* to die in a state of martyrdom, then Stephen Hawking could just as readily have chosen to live in a dual state of being: visible physical weakness and unseen knowledge and power. What if all reality is an illusion?

In any case, it's a good Good Friday whether Jesus died on the Cross or not. He made us believe he died for our sins, and maybe he did. I wonder how he would define our "sins" today. Would he sound like a lefty hippie with New Age beliefs? He certainly was "New Age" in his time. Everything old is new again.

In the pages that follow, I explore the "what if" way of thinking. I've discovered that it has opened up my mind to all sorts of fascinating possibilities. I took events that I believed to be a given and asked myself, "What if . . . ?" I found myself making a whole sequence of subsequent imaginative responses to things I'd taken for granted for years. I changed one historical "fact" and thought about the repercussions that that single difference would have made on all the events that followed.

I let my mind and imagination run free with the "what if" of it all.

My father's favorite speculation was "What if a frog had wings?" His answer: "He wouldn't bump his ass so much."

What if Stephen Hawking could get up and walk? Would the level of his scientific expertise diminish?

I think it probably would, because he wouldn't feel the urge to travel in the cosmos so much.

What if all that we are is simply the result of what we have thought?

What if our daily life itself is an illusion? Our notion of reality is composed only of what we perceive through our physical senses, or what can be recorded by scientific instruments or is commonly agreed upon by consensus. What if all of that is an illusion? What if our *physical* identity programs us to perceive reality in a physical way—that is, in a three-dimensional way? We know there are other dimensions, just as we also know there are higher frequencies than the ones we are able to hear with our ears or see with our eyes.

The truth, as I see it, is that we are multidimensional beings dwelling in many dimensions simultaneously, but we give credence only to what our limited senses impart to us. I believe that our minds influence our physical surroundings because reality is nothing but extended thought anyway. Thought creates form. What we think determines what we experience. Therefore we can change the "reality" of our circumstances by altering our thoughts. I try to remember: thought is the creator of reality.

What if, as quantum physics says, we change what we see simply by observing it? Is that our true power?

What if our parents teach us more than they know—and maybe more than they intend?

My dad was a well-educated teacher who studied for a master's in psychology and philosophy at Johns Hopkins University. He encouraged young people to *think*, not just to pass tests. He used to say that the parents were the problem in the educational system because they didn't encourage their children to think with imagination. (But more than once I heard him proclaim that kids should be put on ice until they were twenty-one!)

He often piled me, my brother, and our mother into the car and drove us to his friend Mr. Palmer's store, over which there was an apartment where the Palmers lived. Dad would park, get out of the car, and head to Mr. Palmer's upstairs living quarters to say hello. The rest of us were left in the car for what seemed like hours at a time but was probably just a few minutes. Sometimes we'd play games with each other, but mostly we learned to observe people passing by—at least I did. Thinking and observing became my entertainment. I never got bored or tired of watching people's behavior and the way they "acted." It seemed to me that they were "acting" their real lives. I think that's why I fell in love with acting as a creative profession. I realized early on that life itself was a kind of chosen performance. But I never enjoyed *becoming* another character. I enjoyed watching myself enact what I thought others would be entertained by. I never lost myself in a character. The thought of letting myself do that is uncomfortable for me because I would have to be so entirely into myself that I would miss seeing the "show business" of life around me. I've never wanted to purposefully lose self-awareness. There's too much entertaining stuff going on that I'd miss. I wouldn't give that up to *become* a character. Observing myself act like someone else is the same feeling I had as I sat waiting for Daddy in the car as a kid, watching people act out their lives. I could feel myself put my whole being in the skin of someone else, but I was still always me, and it was always so satisfying.

At those times, Mother often fell into a reverie of some sort, almost trancelike, which I noticed was a good escape from boredom if there wasn't anything interesting to observe for a while. I developed that trait, too. Whenever I'm with someone who truly bores me, I go into a kind of trance-like meditation, trying to "feel" what they are all about, and usually wander off in thought to another time or place.

I've always believed I've lived other lives, and some of those lives are as real to me now as they were when I lived them. And I've always been comfortable with the notion of other realities and other times coexisting with ours. Einstein and other scientists say that time isn't linear. It is all happening simultaneously. That would mean that all experience is occurring simultaneously. No wonder we all get a feeling of déjà-vu so often. As though there were many personalities inside us, unconsciously remembering experiences from other "times" and places. What if it is normal simultaneously to feel our children as our parents, and vice versa—a reversal of authority roles, so to speak? What if our children feel that, too, and can't understand why?

My father never wanted me to dare too much. He tried to put an emotional fence around me so that I wouldn't venture out in the unknown world and be hurt or possibly so attracted to it that I'd leave home for good. But the emotional fence he erected was not high enough to deter me from jumping over it. So the fence would go up, I'd jump over it, and in effect I soon realized he was unconsciously teaching me how to jump!

But what if his teaching wasn't entirely unconscious?

What if, on some very high level, he knew exactly what he was doing? What if he was schooling me to think with imagination and become a guerrilla traveler, venturing into chaotic, dramatic, sometimes life-threatening situations all over the world so I would understand that the *all* was so much more than I'd been aware of? I've come to believe I was taught to be an avid adventurer by a father who was afraid to leave home and was overcoming his own fears through me.

What if we actually use our close-knit family members to overcome what we've not been able to overcome ourselves? What if my father wanted to spread his own wings—just like that frog—so he wouldn't bump his ass so much? Maybe, in some ways, he gave me my wings.

What if common sense is the collection of prejudices acquired by age eighteen?

—Albert Einstein

What if families are a form of government we either tolerate or revolt from?

What if we didn't have to sleep and dream?

I've always been interested in the reason for sleep. So far, the experts don't have an answer. We need to rest the body and mind, but sleep scientists can't actually prove why. The only thing they can prove is that sleep is necessary for the brain to develop cognitive skills, memory, speech, and innovative thinking.

We know about the stages of sleep: the changes in breathing patterns; the slowing of the heart rate; the delta waves; and the REM (rapid eye movement) sleep, where most dreams occur. During REM sleep, the brain is very active even though we are not conscious. Our bodies are effectively paralyzed, which is said to be nature's way of preventing us from acting out our dreams.

Experts tell us that seven to nine hours of sleep each night are necessary for optimum health. Studies suggest that 27 percent of people are getting fewer than six hours of sleep a night. Lack of enough sleep leads to obesity, chemical disorders, mood disorders, hypertension, depression, anxiety, and congestive heart failure. Maybe lack of sleep is what is wrong with the world!

But what about lack of dreams?

The Bible mentions dreams and the guidance of dreams and visions nearly eight hundred times. Dreams often provide knowledge and forewarning of catastrophes. In Matthew 1:20, Joseph is informed in a dream that Mary is pregnant with Jesus. In Matthew 2:13–14, Joseph is instructed in a dream to leave Egypt with Mary and Jesus to avoid the wrath of Herod.

Our ancient ancestors believed that messages from the gods were delivered in the form of dreams. These communications were considered divine guidance, truths that could heal and solve problems and even bring spiritual wealth, happiness, and understanding to the dreamer. Oracles and priests schooled themselves in the interpretation of dreams. Temples were built as centers of dream worship. The healing energies of the temples soon transformed them into hospitals. It was not unusual for the spiritual seeker to experience a revelation and be fully healed of a physical ailment.

Native Americans believe the Great Spirit delivers to the dreamer visions and guidance for the soul. Dreams can direct us to our true feelings about any aspect of life, from work to love and anything in between. They can warn us of danger or illness, or they can move us in directions we may not have had the courage to explore.

I have friends who lead completely separate lives in the dream state. A woman friend whose beloved husband died says he visits her every single night in her dreams. Therefore, she is never without him. She has never had to adjust to her loss, because he hasn't really left.

Another friend (a man) has lived another entire life in his sleep state for thirty years. In his awake state he is a widower, has three daughters, is retired from the military (he was a colonel), and lives in the desert. In his sleep state he has a wife and children, lives in a forest, and is ten years younger than in his awake state. He tells me his sleep state feels like another time period, and possibly another planet. Every night, he lives inside the dream of his sleep state. He eats with his wife, reads to his children—in a different language, which he understands perfectly. He goes to work, takes walks, and even makes love to his wife. When I ask him if it feels real, he says, "As real as anything here."

Is he reliving a past life, or is he living two lives simultaneously, which is perfectly possible, since *all time is happening at once?*

Dreams can tell us about our present, our past, our future. We can learn about ourselves through dreams. Our dreams are a connection to the divine.

What if our subconscious controls our destiny?

What if the always entertaining Norman Mailer was correct when he argued with me that neurosis is a necessary ingredient in the creation of any kind of art?

We argued about this many, many times. I fancied myself an artistic actress who was basically quite stable, not suffering from much neurotic impairment and quite happy with my level of artistic expression in many areas. While I would never compare my artistic talent to his, I felt he was using his "necessary" neurosis as an excuse to stay neurotic.

Over time, I have amended my views slightly. Perhaps his compulsively outrageous passion for the expression of ideas could be described as neurotic. If so, then, along with finding it entertaining, I would not have liked to see it "cured."

What if our US Big Pharma system is designed to keep people sick rather than cure them?

The last study on this released by Harvard Medical School states that 75 percent of the entire US population is on painkillers! The lines at the pharmacy are longer than the unemployment lines. The pain brought on by disease is being treated rather than disease itself. Why? The drugs are there to disguise the symptoms. As long as a disease remains treatable but is not cured, there is money to be made in pharmaceuticals.

In China the doctors get paid only if the disease is cured. In America the doctors spend most of their spare time educating themselves as to the latest drugs that will help the patient *feel* better. Education among doctors as to the benefits of a healthy diet and acupuncture and natu- ropathic medicine is growing but is not really embraced by the American Medical Association. Why not? Because there is not as much money to be made by the pharma- ceutical drug pushers or by the doctors themselves, who encourage repeated office visits and a regimen of "feel bet- ter" chemicals.

No wonder criminals have shifted from robbing banks to robbing pharmacies—not for money, but for drugs. If Willie Sutton were alive today, he would have to rewrite his motivation for robbing from "because that's where the money is" to "because that's where the 'feel good' is."

I am not a person who understands the addiction to drugs. I've smoked two joints in my life, and each time, I became so hungry I wanted to eat the furniture in the hotel room. I don't like chemically induced ecstasy. I like ecstasy to be more natural. I also loathe taking antibiotics. I real- ize they have at times been helpful to me, but they are not a natural cure, and they are becoming ineffective in many cases. I don't refuse medication on a philosophical basis, but I'd rather face the disease and go right to the root of the problem than treat only the symptoms.

What if the 75 percent of Americans on painkillers sim- ply don't want to know what's actually wrong with them? What if most of our society desires to avoid facing the truth of its existence? What if obesity is an epidemic of comfort food stuffing driven by a desire to avoid recognizing who we have become and how blind we are to it?

What if the so-called war on drugs were shifted from Mexico to the pharmaceutical system right here at home?

We are our own homegrown terrorists.

What if we were as aware of our spiritual nutrition as our physical nutrition?

What if we could all live to ripe old ages of 150, 200, or beyond? What would the Catholic Church's position on overpopulation and birth control and abortion be then?

Perhaps we would have to draw lots on who relocated to the Sahara Desert.

What if negative emotions are what make us sick?

What if we *gain* weight when we diet? Since everything we are is a result of our thoughts, imagine what happens when all we think about is how fat we are.

It's happened to me and many people I know. The body has its own intelligence, and if it thinks it's starving, it will hang on to those calories as long as it can. With every diet I've tried, I've found myself in a battle to the death with my body. It wanted one thing, and I wanted another, because of how I thought of myself, which affected how I saw myself.

I met a Buddhist lama in Bhutan who lived at eighteen thousand feet and ate a little something every two weeks. I climbed to his mountaintop abode. It was a cave—no heat, no running water. His furniture consisted of six statues of Buddha. He sat before them, his legs overlapped in the lotus position. He said he lived on air. He was a "breatharian." He absolutely believed this. I used to watch him descend from the mountain. He seemed to literally float above the ground, using the earth only to propel himself forward. When he reached the frozen lake below, he lowered himself into a hole in the ice and proceeded to meditate until I saw steam rising from his body. He was smiling and serene. When he emerged from the hole, he sat beside the lake in a silent lotus position meditation and levitated a foot or so off the ground. He told me later he had learned to reverse the polarities in his body so that he actually repelled earth's gravity. When he "floated" back up to his Buddha cave, I wondered if I'd dreamed what I'd seen or if I'd seen what I'd dreamed.

Such is the show business of life . . . fat or thin, light or heavy.

What if our allergies are unresolved issues that need clearing?

What if makeup were suddenly illegal? Or if, for some reason, you were told by your doctor that you could no longer wear it? Hard to imagine, since life is show business, and how can you put on a show without makeup?

A recent survey claims that going to work with no makeup causes women more stress than public speaking, or going on a first date, or having a job interview.

In the United States alone, women spend around $7 *billion* on cosmetics every year. And that's just on the face—that $7 billion doesn't even include our hair. A survey of beauticians suggests that 95 percent of us color our hair. When I walked the Santiago de Compostela, the medieval pilgrimage across five hundred miles of northern Spain, I walked alone, carrying a backpack, twenty miles a day for thirty days. On a journey like that, you carry only the absolute essentials with you, and makeup is an unnecessarily heavy item that you do without. I took along with me a small mirror and a small tube of concealer. I thought I would die as, day by day, I watched my hair color disappear to be replaced by gray. (Maybe I should have left the mirror behind, too!) I couldn't remember the last time I'd allowed my natural gray to show itself. I took to wearing broad-brimmed hats, which were necessary anyway, for protection from the sun and the occasional paparazzo. I learned so much about myself on that trip, but one of the little, unexpected things I learned was that I was a committed member of the tribe spending $7 billion on products that I thought I needed to enhance my face on and off the screen.

That was fifteen years ago. One of the liberating parts of aging is I don't really need to care anymore about such things, and so I don't, even when I'm on the screen.

But I'm glad I have my big sunglasses, hair coloring, and wigs. After all, my job is to play many different parts. So those things are job security!

What if beauty is the cure for mental disturbance?

What if women didn't have face-lifts or Botox? Would it help promote equality of the sexes? Would the reality of seeing women's faces as they aged provoke more respect?

Covering what's authentic with a false façade usually means that presentation is being given more value than substance. If a woman cares more about what people see when they meet her than what she does or knows, it shows a weakness in core values and sends a mixed message where equality is concerned.

I never saw a revolutionary, someone agitating for genuine social change, preen with vanity in front of a mirror. That usually happens after they win.

The irony is that wisdom is (or should be) synonymous

with age, not with youth and innocent beauty. So which is more desirable: time and experience leaving no discernible mark on a taut and unmoving face, or time settling in the creases, imbuing that face with outward signs of a life well lived and the wisdom that goes along with it?

I'll go with the latter. And that's because the parts are better in "reel" life *and* in real life. That's equality.

What if aging is all about learning to *love* the fact that nature takes its course?

What if good lighting is the answer to vanity? Stay in the light—in every way.

What if Dick Cheney got a heart transplant from a left-wing, radical hippie, sparking a Jekyll-and-Hyde transformation in reverse? What a movie that would make.

From what I gather, neither Cheney nor his family wants to know the identity of the donor, but the doctors know. Cheney has had five heart attacks, the first at the age of thirty-seven. He was on a heart transplant list for twenty months.

Medical reports say that heart transplant patients often undergo a change of philosophy, personality, and values once they recover from surgery. The heart is a special organ, not to mention one that has tremendous cultural, symbolic, and psychological meaning.

A type A personality and corporate litigator at a top law

firm became more docile, sensitive, caring, and altruistic after his transplant. His tastes in food, music, and books changed completely, corresponding more to the tastes of his donor. The theory of "cellular memory," which says that memories can be stored in individual cells, is taken quite seriously now, and rigorous studies are being conducted into it. The studies indicate that changes in tastes and personality cannot be explained as being side effects of medication or the stress of surgery. They also cannot be explained by recipients getting information about their donors from other sources.

Transplant transference has occurred in many heart recipients. One wrote about her intense cravings for beer, Snickers, and fried chicken—foods she never liked before. Her donor was an eighteen-year-old motorcycle accident victim.

Another transplant recipient, a health-conscious choreographer, found herself inexplicably attracted to all kinds of junk food. She found herself drawn to cool colors instead of the bright reds and oranges she had previously preferred. She also began behaving in an aggressive and impetuous manner that was uncharacteristic of her, but was like the personality of her organ donor.

The end of the Cheney movie could be Cheney telling Kim Jong-un (the Dear Leader in North Korea) to get off the stage of the theater of war because he is too fat, too incoherent, and attracts costars who wear stupid nose rings and too much makeup. All these could be miscast and ill-costumed actors who spout dialogue that doesn't work and who can't act. The new Cheney could persuade news programs to lose interest in war. The audience would walk away. No audience? No ratings. No war.

What if our leaders—in politics, science, philosophy, medicine, and business—actually *led*?

Why don't Putin and Obama lead with honesty and respect for their people's right to know?

Why does the Central Committee in China indulge in a monetary policy that flies in the face of most of the reasons for their People's Revolution in the first place?

Why did Europe forget its glorious multinational history and make the euro its new god?

Why does materialism always ultimately seem to triumph?

When I pose these questions to the people involved, they all tend to reply with the same word: *economics*. Our elections, our art, our scientific exploration, our food, and of course our medical treatment for a sick society—all these are ruled by economics. I see people trudging to jobs they hate, day after day, year after year, wondering why they are alive. Why do they keep doing it? Economics.

The definition of economics is "the theory of production and distribution of wealth." Money has become the foundation of our political system, our supposedly democratic society, and the reason we get up every morning.

How did this happen? When did our lives begin to revolve around money?

I'm no economist. I'm beginning to wonder if anybody is. As a human being with a stake in the game, however, I do feel qualified to speculate on a fundamental cause for the state we find ourselves in. It has to do with the manipulation of Spirituality—which has come to be narrowly called "religion." We as human beings have evolved in such a way that we have allowed ourselves to be separated from God. (When I use that term, I don't mean the God of one particular sect or religion; I mean "the creator of all that is.") Stephen Hawking has told me that a god wasn't necessary for the universe to have been created and to evolve. That notwithstanding (and he may be right), I do wonder how we became separated from the creative force that made everything? How did we get where we are?

More human beings have killed or been killed in the name of a religious god than for any other reason. What in the name of God is going on?

What if God created us and then left it up to us to figure out why?

What if good farmland once again became the most valuable commodity in our world? So much of our land has been decimated by human beings making money out of war.

I live in an area in New Mexico that has some interesting history. In the old days (during the Depression), small farmers grew their own food. There was plenty of water from the river. In small towns, there was a grocery store and a small bar. People were poor. They had little else but land. When someone couldn't pay their bar bill, the owner traded the bar bill for an acre or two of land. Soon the bartender had accrued quite an extensive parcel of land. Those landowners are farmers, and today they may be cash poor, but they are land rich . . . which will bring them cash someday.

What if, in the future, the land with water and nothing else is the beginning of a new, wealthy, food-sharing culture? The last shall be first. The first shall be last. Then all shall be equal.

What if wilderness lands were our new "natural" neighborhoods?

What if shopping makes you greedy? The more you buy, the more you want.

What if ignorance of the truth is the root of all evil?

What if I were married with children, grandchildren, a husband, and a household to run? What if my days were full of grandchildren joking, growing; with youngsters discovering themselves as they played, romped, jumped; with my own grown children, who had brought these little angels to see Grandma (me) so they could feel slightly more relaxed. While basking in my state of well-earned old-age pride, I sit observing them all and holding the hand of my faithful, loyal, hardworking husband and provider of fifty years or so.

No, thanks. I prefer the peaceful rustling trees hanging over my garden wall, one or two adoring dogs, hummingbirds who check in on me, a housekeeper every night for an hour, a diet plan that is FedEx'd to me (thereby avoiding shopping), an iPad so I know what's going on, CNN, fresh-water to drink, a good pair of shoes, and a big hat (shelter from the sun), my books, my paper and pen, my extraordinary memories, and my good friends whom I don't feel compelled to be with.

I live simply and love to be alone to conjure, think, reflect, and have as few responsibilities as possible. I figure everyone is on his own, wrapped in his designed destiny play, which I can't do much about anyway.

After my husband and I split, I made it a point to dodge the marriage bullet. From then on, I had loving sex without commitment. I loved to work hard, and feel I have earned all I have, which is enough for the rest of my life. But mostly I am content. Content with my surroundings, my friends, my family (whom I see when I want to), and my life.

Many women friends my age are finding exquisite peace and happiness on their own. None of us feels alone. On the contrary, we feel free and creative to be who we are. We often have celebratory lunches (too hard to find a parking place at dinner), reveling in our freedom of aloneness.

Wake up, women of the world! You have earned the right to be free of taking care of others. Perhaps it isn't even your *nature*. Perhaps you are the true warriors for peace.

What if marriage is basically a caretaking hedge against death?

What if we really don't understand *love*?

Love, in the biblical sense, is described as the sacrifice of one for another. Here are 140 definitions of love.

1. Someone you'd give your life for;
2. To care more about a person than you care about yourself;
3. Someone you care about more than anything;
4. Friendship;
5. The perfect union of two souls;
6. Family;
7. Patience and understanding;
8. Someone who can make you laugh on your worst day;
9. When you can't live without the other person;

10. Unconditional mutual acceptance;

11. Being there for each other no matter what;

12. Mutual selflessness;

13. Sincere loyalty, affection, and care bestowed without obligation;

14. A feeling of intense sexual desire and attraction toward another;

15. An energy so pure that it makes life want to happen;

16. Being someone's everything;

17. A permanent orgasm;

18. Someone you want to have sex with all the time;

19. A neurological bath of pleasure chemicals;

20. A mutually beneficial symbiotic relationship;

21. The sharing of two lives;

22. Undying devotion;

23. The home you find in someone;

24. Mutual passion and understanding;

25. An unexplainably good and powerful internal feeling;

26. Heaven;

27. A profoundly tender, passionate affection for another;

28. The destiny of two becoming one;

29. A feeling of strong attachment;

30. Having a strong liking or desire for someone or something;

31. A face that is inexplicably attractive;

32. Two hearts beating as one;
33. Inner peace found through (and within) a relationship;
34. An eternal, everlasting feeling of empathy;
35. An agreement between mind, body, and heart;
36. Finding someone who completes your puzzle;
37. That special person that makes everything right in your world;
38. An unbreakable bond;
39. A balance between yourself and the energies of the world about you;
40. Codependent emotional stability;
41. When your mate lets you eat the last bite;
42. A shared, uncontrollable magnetic attraction;
43. I don't know;
44. When you can use the bathroom immediately after someone and not care;
45. Holding hands in the rain without realizing it's raining;
46. An exchange of chromosomal material;
47. Choosing to do what is best for the other person;
48. A state of perpetual bliss;
49. Insanity;
50. An integrated interrelationship beyond the world of the five senses;
51. The fusion of two entities;
52. Stability amid a world filled with chaos;

53. A sense of security;

54. Hanging on to someone no matter what;

55. A spiritual awakening;

56. Saying "I do";

57. Something that keeps itself alive today and its genes alive tomorrow;

58. The exchange of two fantasies;

59. Hot, wild, animal sex in its most carnal state;

60. Two peas in a pod;

61. Making babies;

62. Preeminent kindness or devotion to another;

63. Someone who would never hurt you;

64. Something that conquers all;

65. Something that is blue;

66. A box of chocolates;

67. A dozen roses and a trip to Paris;

68. An extremely stable relationship;

69. A sexual relationship that has stood the test of time;

70. Seeing the truth in another without being afraid;

71. Two souls frozen in time;

72. Not having to wear a condom;

73. Total self-sacrifice;

74. Sharing life's most intimate details;

75. Money;

76. Finding yourself content without any money;

77. The tendency for objects to be attracted to one another;

78. A biological need to procreate;

79. A deep fondness for another person;

80. The transformation of a pair of atoms in a thermo-nuclear reaction;

81. A golden wedding anniversary;

82. Something that makes the world go round;

83. To become one and be happy;

84. A hit from Cupid's bow;

85. The successful seduction of another;

86. An intense emotional state that is based on subjectivity;

87. A biochemical reaction designed to propagate the species;

88. Two bodies entwined in the jungle of life;

89. Dopamine, serotonin, and adrenaline mixed in a blender;

90. A cure for the sickness of life;

91. An addiction resulting in the arrival of offspring;

92. A diamond, 2.5 kids, and a mortgage;

93. Heartfelt gazes into each other's eyes;

94. A home-cooked meal;

95. First impressions, good character, and equal market value;

96. The best days of one's life;

97. The birth of a child;

98. When time stands still;

99. Sexual electricity;

100. The gift of oneself;

101. The sun shining on both sides;

102. The wisdom of a fool;

103. Never having to say you're sorry;

104. Someone to call you darling after sex;

105. A frailty of mind;

106. A pair of twisted souls at peace with their place in the universe;

107. A fool's paradise;

108. Something to do on Valentine's Day;

109. The soul and everlasting foundation for the training of our humanness;

110. A morally powerful mental state;

111. A tie that binds;

112. Something you make instead of war;

113. The inevitable circularity of life;

114. A relationship so close and wonderful that it is bonded by blood;

115. A boy and a girl sitting in a tree K-I-S-S-I-N-G;

116. Taking sides with your mate in any argument with a third party;

117. The tendency to seek one's own benefit or advantage (as in love thyself!);

118. A foot massage, a bubble bath, and Ben & Jerry's;

119. A winged seraph;

120. The pristine integration of twelve fundamental human traits;

121. Winning the hearts of desirable people;

122. An important adaptive decision regarding one's "familial inheritance";

123. The evolutionary propensity toward hetero-zygosity;

124. Survival of the fittest;

125. A thermodynamic equation;

126. Runaway sexual selection driven by a positive feedback mechanism;

127. An exchange of goods in the marketplace of life;

128. The driving force behind the evolution of the human mind;

129. The gateway to immortality;

130. A process designed to eliminate undesirable genetic material;

131. A science to ensure highly pathogen-resistant offspring;

132. The release of virtuous energy in a human chemical reaction;

133. The spreading of high-fitness genes throughout the population;

134. Getting someone to spend vast sums of money on you;

135. A heightened state of activation energy (Ea);

136. Large (negative) values of free energy change (AG);

137. A psychological illusion;

138. A pair of psychopaths playing to deceive each other;

139. The sexual embrace; and

140. A game of chess.

There is hardly any word more ambiguous or confusing than the word *love*. I try to remember, it's not chemistry that gives rise to long-term love—it's thermodynamics!

What if the greatest act of love is to withdraw, allowing another soul to exist?

What if Carol Haney had not sprained her ankle, enabling me, her young understudy, to go on for her in *Pajama Game*?

I believe she and I "chose" the events that occurred. On some level, probably before either of us came along, "it was written." If it hadn't been Carol's accident, another entry ramp for my future would have presented itself.

More important, if I hadn't been prepared when my time came, there would have been someone else warming up in the wings to construct a future of her own. We each have a destiny, a future that is meant for us, but we each also have the power to change that destiny—for better or for worse!—by our actions and by the choices we make every day, and a future in and on the stage of life. Hopefully we play our parts well and with respect for the play we wrote for ourselves.

What if getting a major Lifetime Achievement Award turned out to be like going to your own funeral?

That is the common wisdom. Several actors who have previously won such an award told me it was more a living nightmare than a dream come true. Well, not for me. I found that out when I received the American Film Institute Lifetime Achievement Award in 2012, complete with a star-studded, televised presentation ceremony.

Yes, I was nervous, and I did count the days, but funerals have never been a problem for me anyway, because I believe that no one really dies. I like to celebrate the person at funerals, and make gallows-humor jokes, but none of it is a nightmare. And guess what: neither are lifetime achievement awards. I guess if I thought I didn't deserve the recognition, it would have been a problem, but that sort of false modesty is something I don't relate to.

Let me list the deepest and most profound show business thoughts I had while going through my American Film Institute Lifetime Achievement Award in 2012.

1. What to wear? Should I try to look thin or natural? Thin would mean "She's in great shape for her age." Natural would probably mean more old-lady parts. I opted for natural. I was comfortable, and the outfit didn't look wrinkled when I stood up.

2. Wear a wig or deal with my real hair and pray for good weather? I went with a natural-looking wig, which I knew wouldn't collapse if the weather on the red carpet was hot and moist and windy. The best wigs are not made of natural hair. They are a mixture of synthetic and natural, and therefore keep their shape.

3. Should I wear heels for my entrance to the stage and pray I don't fall going down the stairs to my table? I have a pair of black velvety wedgies. If my gown is long enough, no one will know they aren't dress heels, and my balance will hold. I went with the wedgies. Very good choice.

4. What jewelry? I have very beautiful false diamonds and other stones. Zsa Zsa Gabor got me started on

fake jewelry sixty years ago. "Get mugged for the fake," she said. "You'll still have the real stuff in your safe." I decided on no diamonds or much jewelry of any kind anyway, and earrings the same color as my red-sequined top. My top, by the way, was a $29.95 purchase at a Dress for Less in upstate New York when I forgot to pack performance clothes for a personal appearance a few months earlier.

5. Should I be involved with what clips of my movies should be shown, which of my books should be referenced, which dancing and singing numbers would show why I was being given the award? I had heard stories of others who went before me who were control freaks and spent many hours and days in confused deliberation over what to show. I knew the people in charge of the show were creative and smart. I said to them, "I've lived my life—you interpret it." I offered no particular advice except "Be sure to include the dancing. If you ask me how I would define myself, I would say I'm a dancer who loves to think."

6. Whom should I invite to sit around me at the head table? I don't like putting families on display, so I decided to pay tribute to the actresses in my life whom I admire. Hence: Meryl Streep, Julia Roberts, Kathy Bates, Jennifer Aniston, Barbra Streisand, Melanie Griffith, and Sally Field.

Barbra said yes at first, but then had a conflict in her schedule. Kathy's show got canceled, and she escaped to Europe. (I was furious at her network, who canceled her show saying its ratings were good but that the show appealed only to an older audience.) We emailed often as she helped me through it all. I then decided I wanted my best friend, Brit, and my longtime business manager, Laura, at the table, too.

7. Whom should I ask to speak? I left that task up to people who wanted to do it, knowing how nervous some would be. So some people did, and some didn't. Some of my friends didn't wait for me to ask; they offered: George McGovern, Dennis Kucinich, Carrie Fisher, Jack Nicholson, and my brother, Warren.

8. Which friends in my life should I invite to attend the big night? The invitation I sent actually meant *I'd love it if you were there*. How does one look back over the years and pick those who have meant the most? That's when it rang clear to me just how many had passed on. For a moment, I even wondered if *I* were really still around! I cast my mind back over my politically active years; my writing and publishing career; my Broadway runs, past lovers, Las Vegas days; my Santa Fe friends; my agents, lawyers, New Age confidants, and yes, even that

special someone I spend 24/7 with—my dog Terry.
On a tribute night like the AFI, you want those who
matter the most to you.

I went to a blocking rehearsal the day before the event.
The producers, Bob Gazzale and Christopher Merrill, had
devised a surprise Broadway-style entrance that depended
on a light cue falling on a drumbeat that followed a film
clip of me singing and dancing. I wondered if I could relax
into trusting that it would work and elicit the expected gasp
from the audience.

I trusted.

It worked.

The next night, I arrived for my walk down the red carpet, which I do not enjoy—but Meryl Streep was there to
greet me and walk by my side as the press and photogra-
phers pelted me with shouts and flashes and all-round bed-
lam, something I got over thinking was fun forty years ago.
I'd rather live a quiet, "normal" life, if there is such a thing.
In fact, the definition of "normal" haunted me through the
whole experience.

First, Meryl was like a guiding mother to me. She cared
for me, was sensitive to my age as the lights blinded me,
and made sure I didn't trip. She had been my daughter in
Postcards from the Edge. Now she was my guardian mother.
We posed and acted "natural" for thirty minutes. I felt myself go into a kind of self-generated ivory tower in my head,

where I was in a peaceful and balanced space, acutely aware that the world surrounding me was surreal and possibly dangerous to my health and happiness.

I am basically a loner, and this kind of scrutiny—even though it was a night of celebration—was difficult. I've always been aware in my life that I operate within a show *business* based on contrived fantasy, a business dedicated to making profit from each move and nuance that can be captured on film. This has always made me laugh with wicked recognition. Recognizing the truth of it all has honed in me an ability—and a need—not to reveal in public what I really feel when that's what is required. At times it has been paramount to my survival and to my self-interest. This inner gymnastic was in high gear on the red carpet that night, and I was grateful for the sixty-some years of phantasmagorical experience I've had in mastering the art of self-concealment in public.

As Meryl stood by my side, I thought I could feel her wondering how she would handle the reality of aging so publicly when she reached my age, something that is necessary if one is to survive. It wouldn't be long before she would be playing my parts, a truth not lost on either of us.

I was sustained by the fundamental honesty of our relationship. We truly admire each other. So it was nice to share that publicly in a manner that was also true personally. I thought of how confused audiences often are when it is revealed that people in our business who seem to adore each other on-screen often fight to the death in private. In fact, perhaps we humans are especially gifted with playacting in our lives so as not to be exposed and hurt in front of strangers and loved ones.

I have sometimes been guilty of operating without filters, exposing the truth as I felt it on the spur of the moment, which has sometimes led me to walk right into a snare down the road.

The red carpet finally over, Meryl and I were ushered into the picture-taking gallery, where we were asked to pretend to perform our duties of presentation and acceptance, which would actually occur in another three hours. We did it because we are good actors. I thought, "Is it all about acting to create an emotion in someone else, without regard for what is true and real as it actually happens?" This night would certainly be an example of that.

I didn't know who would be in the audience, who would speak, who would show and who wouldn't, who liked me and who didn't, who would use the platform to remind people they were still working (or weren't but would dearly love to be). Why was I there? Why was this happening? Was it an award for me *and* monetary awards for the American Film Institute? Were we using each other? Why was this such a truth-scouring experience?

The pictures with the AFI board members ended. I was ushered to a last-minute check in a makeup tent peopled with sophisticated hair and makeup experts. I was told if

I needed to go to the bathroom, I should do so *NOW*. Yes, good idea. The bathroom was a Porta Potti. No one could get the door open. Someone kicked it in for me. I entered; the light wasn't working. I pulled down my flowing chiffon slacks and remembered the time my heavy sequined skirt fell into the toilet the night the Thalians gave me an award. Bette Davis drank champagne out of my shoe that night. She didn't care much about me, really, but she sure did care about her ability to give a showstopping live performance. It was wonderful to witness, even though none of it was genuine. What did I expect, anyway? Of course, the whole evening was exquisite pretense wrapped up in pretty make-believe. I was a willing participant, as was everyone else.

My chiffon slacks weren't heavy enough to fall into this toilet. But I couldn't find the zipper head to pull them up and close them. I stood in the dark in the Porta Potti, groping for my zipper while people rapped on the door asking if I was all right, and the audience out front was revving up to take part in yet another evening of Hollywood-style self-appreciation.

All of it for some reason reminded me of the night I, an understudy for Carol Haney in *The Pajama Game,* went on without the benefit of a single rehearsal. This was my recurring dream. I was on and didn't know what to do or what to expect. Was this "funeral" really about my learning to give up control? Maybe I feared that, for me, the opposite of control would turn out to be unmitigated panic.

If there ever was someone who has dedicated her life to living in the present, it is me. Was I about to test that state of being in front of the most famous and talented performers—who would be scrutinizing my appearance, my every movement, for their own purposes? I suddenly realized how impossible it was to experience this event in a simple, straightforward way. Enjoying an evening *all about me* was going to be a trying experience—not really difficult, more uncomfortable. How had I really been feeling about myself over the last forty years or so?

Suddenly they were calling for me on the stage. I left the Porta Potti, my zipper intact. I could hear the music from the film clips. My entrance cue was soon. Someone ushered me in the dark to my mark backstage. I was the prop that needed to be in the right place at the right time for their "effect" to work. That's the way it is in show business. It's all about the show—no, it's really about the business. In any case, if the "effect" doesn't work, you don't get either.

The stage manager counted down to the seven seconds before I needed to walk out in the dark. I counted with him, and then . . . I walked and hit my mark. Boom. The spotlight hit me at exactly the right moment, ignited the stage and the audience. It was technically electrifying. The audience stood up as if on cue and burst into applause . . .

I was on.

I looked out into the audience. The first person I saw was my brother, Warren. He was sitting next to his wife, Annette, whose leg was up on a chair because she had broken her ankle. The pro in me realized he was in the wrong chair, on the other side of the table. So I spontaneously climbed up on his table to get to him. He rescued me by lunging across the table and sweeping me into his arms. "I love you," he whispered as the audience clapped harder.

I wondered if Mother and Dad were looking down on this moment in pride. Or had they always wanted such recognition for themselves? Warren had received his own AFI Lifetime Achievement Award a few years earlier. And when we publicly embraced then, the audience collectively sighed, "Aaahhhhh."

I knew Warren and I were a remarkable success story in Hollywood. Had there ever been a brother and sister like us? There'd been sisters—Olivia de Havilland and Joan Fontaine. And father and son—Kirk and Mike Douglas. But another brother and sister? Not that I could think of. I've always been moved to write about our parents. Warren elected to keep his early private life private. But when the two of us appear anywhere together, especially in celebration, questions about our mother and father immediately seem to come up.

Mother had wanted to become an actress, and Dad was a homespun but sophisticated mystic and philosopher who played the violin and once told me he had wanted to run away and join the circus. Had I seen these qualities in them and attempted to fulfill their unrequited dreams by making them happen for myself? These days, my long-term memory is one of the only things operating as well as it ever did, and I find my mind speeding back to little scenes and events in our childhood that could offer a clue to how we became who we are . . . yet it all seemed so middle-class normal to me. Nothing dramatically stimulating, really. No particularly deep sadness, drama, or, for that matter, pressure to succeed. I remember my childhood mostly as an exercise in not upsetting the neighbors. What they might think of us was a matter of great concern in our house. Perhaps such a concern is the prime prerequisite for a show business career: *What will the people think?* We play for the audience.

Then I realize that probably everybody is subtly educated for the same priority: live and work according to what the audience wants; always consider what the neighbors might think. Probably that is why everyone in Hollywood often seemed so nervous: it's a town where your "neighbors" are also your competitive peers.

Had Warren followed my lead because I was older and unabashedly certain of my own destiny in show business? Our seventy-five-plus years together culminated in this moment, as though it had been ordained by an unknown force. I remember one time he slipped and fell, and I picked him up. I remember how I told him how brilliant he was and that he should live up to that and not waste any more time. We were sitting in New York City at P.J. Clarke's, and when he got up from the table I could feel his future concretize.

I eased away from his embrace, knowing I should respect the audience and get on with wading through the standing, smiling, applauding guests to my table. I wondered if they had brothers or sisters who wanted to be standing where they were.

The people of my past surrounded me. I wanted to stop and embrace every one of them, but I was aware that I shouldn't take too long. I passed and hugged Bobby Harling, the writer of *Steel Magnolias* and director of *The Evening Star*. We had been through an awful lot together, which, thank goodness, he kept to himself, and thus became known to me as The Tomb. Larry Mark had produced *Terms of Endearment* and was famously adept at understanding complicated, brilliant directors, namely Jim Brooks, one of my favorite people. Larry once figured out that if he wanted me to agree to be cast in one of his productions, he should contrive to make it seem like doing so was my dog's greatest desire. The road to my heart was through Terry, and even if it meant making her my costar, Larry was willing to do it. However, when he tried to implement his strategy and pitch the film to me, he failed to remember that Terry was a "she" and referred to her as "he" the entire time. Once he realized his error, he fell apart laughing. "Oh my God—I fucked up with the dog. Now I have no recourse," he blurted out.

I embraced George McGovern, who had literally left his hospital bed to be with me that evening. I remembered the two years I gave up all my work to campaign for him because I felt Richard Nixon would be the ruination of America's authenticity and respect in the world.

I circled around when I saw Dennis Kucinich. We had been friends for nearly forty years, since he was the boy mayor of Cleveland who took on the Mob. I went through his divorce with him and was the godmother to his daughter, and a follower of his political career, and admirer of his liberal views on foreign policy. He was out of politics now, having lost his last election, and we had been discussing launching some kind of global spiritual initiative, which needed financing.

My world was diverse and varied. Across from Dennis was Don Rickles. Rickles had been a mainstay in my Vegas days. Often he and Dean and Frank and a handful of others would sit around my backstage dressing room cracking jokes until six in the morning. I have been on Vegas time ever since. The Rat Pack was actually first dubbed "The Clan," which came from a *Life* magazine article written when we did *Some Came Running* together. The journalist just nicknamed us The Clan, which was okay with us. But over the years, our group's name became confused with that of the Bogart-led group called the Rat Pack. And that was okay, too.

When I hugged Rickles, I realized we were the last living renegades of that time, and Don was about ten years older than me. Those days were a celebration of the unruly, unearthed, untouched, underestimated, childlike talent for fun in all of us. For me, the prime example was the day I pointed and shot a toy water pistol at Sam Giancana, and he pulled out and pointed a real .45 at me. Dean and Frank broke out in uncontrollable giggles and threw jelly beans at both of us. More than anything in my life, I miss experiencing episodes of spontaneous, fun insanity in the company of profoundly talented people who were powerful enough to tell the powers-that-be to take a hike.

I made my way to the table hosting my Santa Fe family. They had piled themselves onto planes to experience the glamour of Hollywood and, even more, to be there for me, just as they always were at home. In Santa Fe, we were there for each other—far from the lights and din of show business.

I made the decision to move out of California some years ago. I wanted to live in a place where your perceived value as a person didn't rise and fall depending on weekend box office receipts or what table you got at a restaurant, and I wanted to spend my time closer to nature than to traffic. Santa Fe was a natural choice for me because it is the spiritual capital of the country. There are more psychics, channelers, past-life therapists, shamans from Indian tribes, naturopaths, homeopaths, and artists there than anywhere else in the world. New Mexico is also the backyard playground for UFOs. I think it's because the crystals in the ground amplify human consciousness to a higher level of spiritual understanding, something that has been a particular study of mine for fifty years. All of it is "normal" for me. Santa Fe and nearby Abiquiu were natural places for me to settle, and I've been very happy there. I feel that I have a kind of perfect life—Santa Fe, Abiquiu, Malibu, and sometimes a week or two in New York and wherever I go on location to make a movie. American Eagle has nonstop flights from Santa Fe to L.A., which makes it like a private airline for me and Terry and my new dog, Buddy-Bub. (More on Buddy-Bub later.) I embraced everyone at the Santa Fe table, knowing the famous faces in the room had no idea who they were.

Then I approached the head table. There sat all these women I treasured and admired. I knew I should move from one to the next swiftly, because I could easily have stopped and had an hour-long conversation with each one. Then, arriving at my seat in the center of it all, I motioned for the audience to finally sit down. Show business people know how to keep the illusion going, but they usually need some direction as to when it's okay to stop.

The show began. Howard Springer, the head of the AFI, came to the center of the stage, took the microphone, and immediately made a joke about my having lived so many lives that it was hard for them to concentrate on one. Not only did the audience not laugh, but half of them booed. I was glad. Thank goodness there was going to be some editing for the broadcast that would run on the TV Guide network. He then made a worse joke, about a friend of ours who was using us both as excuses to arrange parties. I was embarrassed for him and for our friend, but grateful that Howard refrained from naming him.

I had wondered how my friends who had chosen to speak would decide to handle the potential for humor inherent in my well-known beliefs in reincarnation, UFOs, and the like. The audience had put the room on notice. If it's *really* funny, okay. Otherwise—don't go there.

The fundamental meaning of freedom of speech, the First Amendment, always comes out with an audience of people who represent the spectrum of humanity. This audience was a testing ground for truth in good and lousy taste. Just because we're free to say something doesn't mean we should say it. As far as I could recall, jokes about somebody's deeply held spiritual beliefs had not really been attempted in Big-Time public before. Because I had been so open about mine, the comedy people felt welcome to take a shot at being funny with spiritual material. I was interested to see how they fared. I had always told people to feel free to make jokes, just make sure they're funny. But how do you make reincarnation funny? You have to be Jack Black.

Somewhere near the top of the show, they showed a film clip written by and starring Jack Black, and for which he'd even done the wardrobe and makeup. He appeared as a caveman, a monk, an extraterrestrial, and a beaver trapper. In each sequence, he spoke as a character out of one of my lifetimes, giving detailed comedy riffs about what had gone on in a cave, in a church, on another planet, and in a cabin.

Everyone in the room, including me, laughed so hard, because it was hysterical and because we were relieved he'd hit the nail on the reincarnation comedy head early. If you are going to do those kinds of jokes, you have to attack them comedically hard. He did. In fact, he was so funny that I could feel others, including me, mentally strike whatever funny joke we'd planned to attempt. When Jack Nicholson got up, he said he had a *great* joke, but "after Jack Black, I'd rather go out and bury the motherfucker alive for making it impossible for anyone else." We all applauded. We were off the hook!

For me, the hidden risk in the evening was how people would handle the material in my books. Other recipients had controlled *everything* that was said, but that's not how I operate.

As the evening progressed and people spoke, the speeches tended to focus on things such as my "audacity" and "courage to be myself." Speakers said it didn't matter what my belief system was. It was the public expression of what I believed that seemed to impress and inspire people. I had never realized how much.

My brother, Warren, started the evening, introducing many people at their tables, then leaned forward and said, "I am here to honor a person I have loved every single day of my life." He said it as a kind of pronouncement and with such directed force that I knew he was close to dissolving in tears. I was, too.

When Jack Black said, "Getting the AFI Lifetime Achievement Award is a Big Fucking Deal," it was the simple truth. More important than any Oscar (although one of these helps), because it's about your work throughout your whole life, not just one performance.

Anyway, I brought myself back to the present, and when John Travolta walked out, showing he had the courage to overcome his current problems involving tabloid exploitation to be there for me, I remembered that my real task that night was to *appreciate* what was happening and to revert back to nervousness as to what the neighbors would think. John had it right. Above all, I was a dancer—hence team player—disciplined, hardworking, and somewhat accustomed to pain and criticism. He said, "Don't worry about me and the press. I'll be in and out. I want to do something for *love*." John is a prince of principles and a friend forever.

Julia Roberts, who was seated at a table with her cameraman husband and family, came to sit with me when the show started, understanding that the pictures of herself and Meryl on either side of me would be the image the audience could remember. She ran her reincarnation joke by me and asked if she should say it. I said, "You heard their reaction to Howard Stringer. Save yourself the embarrassment." She agreed, and when she spoke, she said she admired me because I had balls. I had balls, she continued, because I had told certain members of the Mob to go screw themselves. I loved that she told the story, but it was cut from the TV version. I loved the contrast between the spiritual belief in re-incarnation juxtaposed with the Mob, who kill people who really don't die. No one would get that but me—but never mind.

Dakota Fanning, whom I met when she was eleven years old, came out in her full-fledged teenage glory. She spoke of the time we'd spent together for a magazine article on Hollywood. I was pleased that her mother had left the two of us alone back then, and Dakota herself seemed so normal, not suffering from any of the side effects of show business fame. She gave me a bracelet, which I still have. I remembered myself at eleven, doing handstands in the backyard, and wanting only to be a good dancer, and going to see every available movie at the Bellevue Theater in our neighborhood. Would her future be similar to mine? And I learned her younger sister wanted to be an actress, too. Two sisters vying for the same parts—I was so glad Warren was a boy!

Mike Nichols appeared on the screen. He knew exactly what had motivated my acting—it was dancing. He said I had the soul of a dancer because I understood pain. He said my walk conveyed what was on my mind. I remembered how often we talked about karma when we shot *Postcards from the Edge*. He was interested in the "otherness" of real-ity and was curious to speculate even further. Mike is a ge-nius director because he was also an actor (part of the great comedy team Nichols and May). He understands levels and aspects of performing in a way that only one who has done it can. I was honored that he took the time to offer a tribute to me.

When Morgan Freeman stalked across the stage and said, "I didn't *have* to be here. I *wanted* to because movies matter and so does she," I remembered the flirt fest we had during one publicity marathon. He was drumming his fingers on the lunch table, and I told him I would like to be the top of the table and under his thumb. He smiled and played the rest of the day for what it was worth. During his speech, he went on to remind the audience that movies change us as individuals and collectively as a people, and I was part of that change. I still wished I could be a tabletop he'd drum on.

I had never met Katherine Heigl. She had come, she said, to pay tribute to what I had done for women. She was very serious in front of such a crowd of luminaries, acknowledged that fact, and then leaned into the microphone and asked for my autograph. I signed the air in front of me.

Dennis Kucinich had come all the way from Washington and spoke of our thirty-five-year friendship and our mutual contemplations on other realities. I remembered his face during the presidential campaign when Wolf Blitzer asked him if he really had seen a UFO from the balcony of my home in Washington State. I held my breath for his answer. When he said, "Yes, I did," I couldn't have been prouder of our friendship. But then the audience laughed, and I once again understood that humiliation had become the most significant tool of disinformation. Why would anyone who has an empathetic bone in his body want to seriously speculate as to whether we are alone in the universe if he were only going to be laughed at? Then, for the record, Dennis recovered the moment by saying, "It was an Unidentified Flying Object. I don't know what it was." I guess it was one step forward and half a step back.

The UFO that he and two other people witnessed that night had produced a sense of awe in him that still resonates when he speaks of it. We met at Elaine's restaurant in Manhattan thirty-five years ago, with Bella Abzug as our common friend. Tonight he lovingly spoke of my intellectual curiosity and called for everyone to applaud to show their compassion for those who take inner-truth journeys—namely, me. I love him so. He said I made life an art form.

Misha Baryshnikov said he had studied everything he could about me because he was interested in how I had handled Khrushchev when the Russian premier came to visit the set of *Can-Can*. Khrushchev had said, "The face of humanity is prettier than its backside." I replied, "He was just upset because we wore panties." (In France, the home of the provocative can-can, the dance was done without underwear.) Reminiscing about the making of *The Turning Point,* Misha said he had loved the on-set jousting between Anne Bancroft and me, almost like dancers. I remembered how exhausting he found the length of time in between takes, as the lighting was perfected. He said, "I'd rather do two full-length *Swan Lakes*. It's less tiring!" While shooting *The Turning Point,* I deeply understood that I was watching the capturing of the greatest dancer of all time on film. Take after take, always perfect placement, perfect execution, perfect stamina. Two full-length *Swan Lakes* would have been nothing for him.

Sally Field, even with all her success, was so adorable. She talked about our time on *Steel Magnolias,* with its female bonding. What she didn't mention was that we partly bonded over our dislike for our director, Herb Ross. He was an ex-choreographer, and therefore adept at cruelty, being particularly unkind to Julia, Dolly, and Daryl. Sally was too big a star for him to bother, and I was on to him. Sally said I was so interested in her that I even made *her* interested in herself. She said I helped her with her crying scene by suggesting she just stick menthol in her eyes—that would help her cry. Then there was Don Rickles. He started by saying, "The fish course sucked." (He was right.) He looked at the famous crowd and said, "I don't need you people. I won't kiss ass like you've been doing all night." He said the evening was eighteen long hours of crap. He looked at Jack Nicholson and said, "I know you'd rather be oiling the Lakers' jocks." Nobody understood better than Don that famous people love for the mickey to be taken out of them. We all doubled over in laughter. He looked at Warren and said, "Of course you want the evening to be about *you* again."

Don was sitting with a married couple who were two major donors to the AFI. They had asked to be seated at his table. Don turned to them and said, "I'm sitting with some rich Jew and a wife with a bad nose job." They also doubled over in laughter.

He went on to mention that he'd never read any of my books and didn't plan to. He turned to Julia Roberts and said they lived near each other at the beach, but of course she wouldn't deign to acknowledge him. She started to speak, and he shot back, "Shut up. You have no lines." Again, hysterical laughter.

I had wondered what Don would do with this crowd when he asked to speak. I told him, Kid around with anything you like, especially my beliefs. He opted to take his shots at the fame gathered in the room instead. Very smart. At the end of his rap, he said I made a person feel they were loved.

By now I was having a whale of a good time. Who had said it was like going to your own funeral? Who had told me it would be a nightmare?

Jack Nicholson got up, and after he made the "I'd like to bury him" remark about Jack Black, he said three things I'll never forget: "You madly love your audience," "Both your body and your body of work have long legs," and "You are completely available and forthcoming while remaining a mystery." So well observed.

Then came Meryl, whom I had asked to present me with

the award because she is simply the best in the world. She said, "Everything about her turns up—her eyes, her mouth, her attitude, her nose, and her outlook." She said I had the stamina of a teenager, and what she admired the most was that I'd had my biggest successes in my middle years, giving hope to all women as they grow older. She said she loved seeing me on the screen because I felt so privileged to be there.

I felt privileged to know her and everyone else who had made that night so memorable. I wouldn't mind having more funerals like that one.

What if our friends are our best teachers because there is only sharing without expectation of anything in return?

What if I don't know anything about acting on the screen?

Truth is, I don't. I have no idea how it happens for me. I have no techniques, no practices, no commandments.

I read the script once. I get a "feeling" for the subject and the character, and immediately I either "see" myself doing the part or I don't. I usually don't seriously read the script again until the night before the first day I work.

I don't totally memorize my lines until I get on the set, because I associate the lines with the movements I make. Being a dancer at heart, when I move around in a scene, I know what to say and when to say it. I "see" myself. The character's body language dictates to me what the makeup and wardrobe and hair are going to be. The picture becomes increasingly clear to me, and that's all I need. I hear the rhythm of speech and see the movement of my head and hands and arms. Usually I stop these mind pictures before they get too specific, because I want to wait and see who else will be appearing in the scene with me. Then I just pay attention . . . I listen to and watch what the other actors do. *That* adds another layer to how I will play my part.

I love it when the other actors are brilliant. I meld myself into their talents, something like what I do in real life when I'm with a really interesting person. I love to observe people and their behavior, which I'm sure comes partly from all the hours spent sitting in the car watching people while I waited for my dad to come back. Observing and participating in a scene with really good actors is one of the greatest pleasures in my life. That's probably why so many of us fall in love with our costars. We truly believe the romance is happening to us. And doing scenes over and over, perfecting the reality of it all, is sometimes better than interacting with people in real life, because there's no authentic past involved, nor an anticipated future.

On a set, there is sometimes competition between what the leading man wants and what the male director wants from an actress. Both are vying for the love and attention of the leading lady, and the leading lady is doing the same thing in reverse. In the end, everyone, from the actors to the crew, wants to please the parental figure: the director. And when all is said and done, we want to please and be accepted by the audience.

What if a film set were like a mini nation-state?

Here's how it would be organized: The director is the (hopefully) benevolent ruling dictator; the actors and crew and writers represent the varied levels of craftsmanship and art among the professional citizenry; the set is everyone's home country; and makeup, hair, and wardrobe people do the hard work of making us look like we actors belong together in this place. Unfortunately, the producers and financiers are the people who make all of it possible or not. Maybe they feel like they are God in my analogy!

The underlying humanity of a film set is a combination of hypersensitivity and a pristine, almost puritanical work ethic. Time is not to be wasted, because time is money, but very often it's necessary to stop, take a deep breath, and realize that the authentic depiction of human emotions is the true reason why we're there. If we don't emulate human comedy and drama accurately, we won't have a success.

Real secrets are kept and rarely gossiped about. Personal idiosyncrasies are shared, tolerated, and usually celebrated as entertaining.

The financiers of independent productions have to visit the set so they can understand where their money is going. Sometimes they stand behind the "video village" monitors and "suggest" changes to the director. If the actors hear that, they either laugh or go to their trailers and waste some time. In the old, studio days, the front office saved its suggestions for a more discreet private time with the director. They knew more about what the distributors and the public wanted anyway. And they were the dreamers of the financial art who listened to their profit-driven better angels. Today the indie producers feel "artistically compelled" to raise the money to "express themselves" at a film festival and to hang out with stars.

Money is raised by selling off distribution rights in foreign territories, the value of which is determined by how bankable a film's stars are in any given country. The big studios are interested in "branded" projects: *Spider-Man 13, Aliens vs. Humans on Mars, Robot Creep King, Son of Robot Creep King* . . . etc., etc.

The independent film industry is where the awards are, because the scripts are better, not branded, and more original. But there's rarely money in independent films. Nonetheless, to me, movie dream-making is still the most awe-inspiring form of expression I know of. The fact that it's also a business is just something we have to tolerate. And all of it is Show Business. There are two businesses in the world. Everyone else's business and Show Business.

What if live theater reminds us that we all live on a stage, and we need to get our parts right?

Retakes are a luxury available only in the make-believe world of film.

What if Broadway were just a nothing street and not a place where performers get to work in front of a live audience?

Here's what I think about when I remember performing on Broadway.

The theater was packed. The audience represented all ages. I had put together a medley of songs that required me to act out a disappointing but ultimately exhilarating love affair. I knew I couldn't sing that well, so it all depended on my acting the songs. I could hear the audience chuckling when it was funny. That inspired me to completely open myself to try new acting expressions in between the notes. The emotion of the music enveloped me, and then I enveloped the audience. Then there was a long, silent beat before I changed emotions

in the middle of the stream . . . the audience went with me. It
was utter magic.

The experience of a live audience is the ultimate in karmic interplay. What you put out, you get back. I came to
understand why the Greeks said that live theater was an exercise in touching your "godhead" for both the performer
and the audience. It's because everything and everyone becomes *one*.

To me, that's the essence of spirituality.

Whenever I played Las Vegas and heard the tinkling of
ice in whiskey glasses, I knew I didn't have them or the godhead. How to repair the tinkling into silence is the task of
one who wants to be totally in his or her godhead.

The theatrical electricity of human appreciation is like no
other, particularly the moments of silence. There is a rever-
ence in the silence for work well done. The audience ab-
dicates its identity and communicates from the heart as it
reacts to what it sees and hears. The silence is breathtak-
ing. I am fascinated at how our leaders and politicians understand perfectly that the art of swaying a live audience is
their success or failure. They ask some of us for lessons in
accomplishing the command of an audience. But of course,
we can't help them. It's an innate act of openhearted sharing.
How can you share openheartedly when you are worried
about numbers and money?

A child can walk on a stage and the audience obeys—or a dog, or any living being who simply stands there doing nothing and staring into the collective eye that waits. Oscar Hammerstein called the audience the Big Black Giant. Is it there to judge you or to celebrate with you?

I suffer from stage fright still, and try to regard the audience as my Gigantic Friend. But when all is said and done, the need to please an audience must come from needing to be loved. People who have had enough love and attention in their childhoods are usually no good on the stage.

I wonder, would political leaders be less effective in their wheeling and dealing if they had had enough love as children?

What if the theater left audiences in touch with their own God spark?

I say, when it works, it does.

What if I hadn't said yes to joining the cast of *Downton Abbey*?

Being involved with *Downton* has been one of the great pleasures of my "mature" years, and quite unexpectedly it seems to have provided me with a new identity to the public! More people come up to me and tell me how much they enjoyed seeing me in *Downton Abbey* than they do for just about any feature film I've ever made.

My experience shooting *Downton Abbey* was a lesson in living in the past and in an extreme form of materialism: I was enacting a period when a rigid class system kept an iron grip over society's mores and attitudes. Social status and personal wealth trumped everything else, including character and intellect.

My first day of filming, I arrived on the exterior set of Highclere Castle as a damp mist was falling. The servants stood at attention according to their rank in the household. I emerged from the vintage car and stood on its running board, striking a period kind of pose, which I thought would be appropriate, and it induced a familiar kind of flashback memory for me.

Had I experienced something like this before?

The castle rose into the shrouded sky. I knew it had been completely rebuilt by an early Lord Carnarvon during the height of the Victorian era. One of his descendants, another Lord Carnarvon, was the famous amateur Egyptologist who, with English archaeologist Howard Carter, unearthed King Tut's tomb. Many of the artifacts Lord Carnarvon and Howard Carter discovered in Egypt had been sold to the Metropolitan Museum of Art in New York, but I'd read that not too long ago the family had uncovered another cache of objects from ancient Egypt that had apparently been hidden in a cupboard somewhere in the castle. They were now on display in the castle's basement. To tell the truth, I was looking forward to discovering whether the place was haunted.

As the cameras rolled, the actors playing servants waited at attention for me to approach. One by one I addressed them, and they smiled at me in a highly controlled manner. Then I walked into the castle. The entryway ceilings were so high that they reminded me of the Vatican. A winding staircase rose to my right and my voice, along with those of the other actors, echoed across the halls. The rugs were works of art under my feet. They were splashed down upon teakwood floors that intermittently echoed with our footsteps as well. I was in another world, but one that felt peculiarly familiar. That didn't surprise me. I was probably going home to a house like the fictional Downton Abbey from another time! I entered the formidable dining room. The table was the length of a small runway and was decorated with crystal and cutlery and china out of a royal display. An expert in royal protocol serving as a technical adviser stood guard by the table. He observed every detail of our behavior with military precision and told us in no uncertain terms what was permitted and what was not. (He was actually a very nice man.)

Original paintings spanning three hundred years of art history hung on the walls, a Turner and a Van Dyck among them. I was told some of them would fall from the walls if "they" became upset at anything occurring within "their walls" of protection. I didn't understand *who* would be upset, but I knew better than to ask.

I remembered that the British Society for Psychical Research, which began in the 1880s, was the organization that was home to the most celebrated and sophisticated of researchers into such matters. In the glory days of Highclere Castle, Sir Arthur Conan Doyle (the creator of Sherlock Holmes and Watson) and his circle were among the most famous scientists of the "paranormal," which to me was rapidly becoming normal. I wondered if they had ever graced this very table.

I gazed at the table, imagining what it would have been like to participate in discussions about Egyptian pharaohs and their larger significance. Was Lord Carnarvon looking for more than the golden treasures of a pharaoh's tomb? Did he have an idea that what he found in Egypt might also relate to the missing link in human history? Did he speculate on the possibility of extraterrestrial involvement in making the human race what we are today? Were the Egyptian pharaohs star visitors themselves who understood reincarnation as a truth, and whose literal-minded subjects buried them with their treasures so they'd have something to come back to? Were aspects of their hieroglyphs actual descriptions of their off-world home? Maybe the walls of this dining room still resonated with the sound frequency of some of those long-ago speculations and discussions. I wondered if people a hundred years ago made jokes about such speculations or if they were more scientifically serious in their quest for answers.

There would be many days spent seated around this table for me and the extraordinary cast of *Downton Abbey*. We waited there in between setups, gossiping about our lives, politics, royals, the state of the economy, and life itself.

On that first day, at one point I heard a buzzing among the cast and I turned around. There was Maggie Smith walking toward me. My God, she could be hysterically funny even as she simply put one foot in front of the other. We are almost the same age (well, she is eight months younger than me). She laughed out loud when she saw me, and we embraced. She reminded me that we had first met forty years earlier, backstage at the Oscars. We were standing next to the catering table. I was up for an Oscar and when they announced that someone else had won, she recalled, "You tucked into the chocolate cake on the catering table and said 'Who cares about being thin anyway? Fuck it!'" Maggie still remembered that backstage conversation forty years later.

We spent many hours sitting together on the set of *Downton* reminiscing about men, work, the world as it used to be. It was easy because neither of us particularly likes to get up and walk around anymore. One day, I told her that for one particular scene we were going to be filming, I would serenade her with a rendition of "Let Me Call You Sweetheart." I asked her how she was going to react. She said, "I'm going to fall asleep in my chair." Then she said, "No, I'm going to laugh in your face." Then she said, "No, I'm going to throw up!"

In the end, she giggled and curled up like a schoolgirl and looked utterly adorable. Wise choice—Maggie stole the scene from me.

While dressing for my first scene, I realized it was impossible to do so without the help of at least one servant and possibly two. The buttons (totally authentic) were too small and located somewhere on the back of the garment, and there seemed to be hundreds of them. I could never have gotten dressed by myself. The corset alone would have prevented a woman from reaching around to fix a button on the back of her dress. The shoes were so narrow (and exquisite) that I needed a gentleman helper to walk. No wonder clothing styles changed as the *Downton* world of lady's maids and valets disappeared. Without a maid, it would have been literally impossible for a woman to dress in an "appropriate" manner—much less do so several times a day, as the well-to-do women of that era did. As long as wealthy women had their maids, designers were free to indulge in these creations. Once the maids disappeared, so did that particular style of dress.

Everything we touched was authentic—the props, hats, furs, chairs, lamps—everything. We were not allowed to sit in the drawing room. A makeshift "other" room was set up with beach chairs and bottles of water. The actresses sat around in their corsets, which I had refused to wear. They were composed, comfortable, and ready for the rest of the day's work which would occur outside, *in the rain*. No problem.

There we played the scene as the wind and rain blew around and on us. The English actors didn't seem to notice the weather. They plowed straight ahead. I tried not to notice it, either, but I was freezing, and the dog in the scene (whose name was Abbey!) couldn't get it right. We did the scene over and over. The actors were disciplined and perfect each time. I was impressed. But what struck me more than anything was how unaware they seemed to be of the fact that their show was the biggest TV hit in the world. It was as though they were living in the *Downton Abbey* universe and the rest of the outside world was unknown to them. Perhaps that was the correct mind-set to establish in order for authenticity to permeate the performances. I also believe that part of the success of *Downton* is that Julian Fellowes has structured a wonderfully old-fashioned story with the attention span of the Internet age in mind: we never spend too much time with the same characters, the scenes are always short and fast-paced, and there are so many story lines being juggled that nobody watching could possibly get bored.

We weren't allowed to view any takes on the monitor, but everyone trusted the director implicitly. Besides, it was TV, and there was no time to wait for the rain to stop or the scenes to be perfected. I was having a very high-class English acting experience.

In my scenes with Maggie Smith, I was in heaven. Her timing, of course, was impeccable, as we batted our dialogue back and forth like veteran Ping-Pong players. When I sang "Let Me Call You Sweetheart" to her, it was as though she were my girlie lover. In fact, months later, when I was asked at the *Downton Abbey* press conference if I had known Dame Maggie Smith before, I said, "We were lovers in another life."

I spent two and a half weeks shooting my part. I had a

wonderful driver who put me back in touch with the British working class after a day among the swells. He took good care of me. I stayed in an inn where, they say, Richard III had slept in my bedroom. The ceilings were so low I felt compelled to hunch over, and the uneven stone floors and narrow, winding staircase leading to my room tested my balance.

In some ways, it was a complicated shoot for me. I was beginning to confront the realities of aging without the comforts of home, while at the same time trying to fit into an English period piece as an American woman who was advocating for change in the *Downton* household.

I missed my dog Terry every day, and particularly every night. I love cuddling up to her, and now I had no one to put my arms around. I received pictures of her on my iPad every day from the friends I had entrusted to take care of her. I thought often about how all humans can experience a deep and true love for an animal. I dreaded the day in the future when she would pass on. I seriously doubted I would be able to walk into my house were I not to find her there, jumping into my arms. You think of these things when you're on location in a faraway place. You come to realize what is most important in your life at home. Yes, it's a foreign adventure, but I was longing for the sameness and routine habits of home. In fact, I began to understand the comfort of tradition the characters in *Downton Abbey* cherished. My character was a contradiction to what I was feeling personally. Acting in good scripts always makes me understand life more.

I now began to speculate what I would do if and when they asked me back to *Downton*. Terry would be almost fourteen by that time. I could fly her with me to the United Kingdom. But would there be a required quarantine before getting her back into America (bird flu protection)? I wished Julian Fellowes would write a season in which the *Downton* family comes to America. I would stay on the show as long as they wanted. But I knew Maggie wouldn't travel to America. Our verbal jousting was why they wanted me in the first place. Oh my . . .

I should stop speculating on the future. *Now* was what was important. I went to the opulent dining table, sat with my actor friends and colleagues, and told them, upon request, about my days with the Rat Pack, Wilder, Wyler, and one of their own: Hitchcock! It was good to be telling these old stories from my life in the present.

I had a feeling *Downton Abbey* would be part of my life for a long time to come. Perhaps I really had lived in the 1920s and had traveled to this very castle and that's why it was all so familiar to me.

What if there really is reincarnation?

What if sex is only a chemistry experiment?

What if sex isn't meant to be monogamous?

I've lost count of how many people already agree with this. Yet in show business, what sells best of all usually involves a story of infidelity.

One of Masters and Johnson's and Kinsey's many investigations into human sexuality turned up results that I found fascinating. The questions they asked of thousands of people were quite objective, based on the subjects' daydreams, fantasies, specific behavior and activities, and unrequited desires. They concluded that human beings basically fall into one of three categories: one-third of us are monogamous, one-third of us are promiscuous, and one-third are serially monogamous. They also found that on a scale of 0–6, with 0 being exclusively heterosexual, and 6 being exclusively homosexual, about 96 percent of us are a 3!

I found this perfectly in alignment with the desires of the soul in human beings. From my studies, the soul is an equal balance of yin and yang—feminine and masculine. Over many lifetimes, our soul identity has experienced both male and female incarnations, so that we can learn the values and traumas of each. "All of the above" then is the true sexual identity of each of us. Bisexuality is just a part of it. In other words, when considering sexuality, there is much more to factor in than simply male and female and the preferences of each. Within the landscape of androgyny are sexual preferences we've probably never even contemplated. Since sexual activity is both a tool for the expression of one's identity and the means of procreation, the creativity and diversity it encompasses must be without boundaries.

My sexual adventures and preferences are more subdued now—and were never truly outrageous. I'm sorry, because I wonder what I would have discovered in myself had I grown up in a liberated and imaginative environment. Living in a way that resonated with the androgynous nature of my soul would have been an entertaining and self-revelatory adventure. I often wonder what sex is like for highly advanced ETs who are technologically and spiritually superior to us. What if being "superior" isn't even a level of intelligence but only a mark of the experience earned by longevity? What if the only thing that counts is creativity—in matters sexual and otherwise?

What if monogamy went out of style? Would spouses cheat if it were accepted behavior?

Show business would be in trouble without its favorite source of dramatic tension.

What if Spiritual Hunger is what we are suffering from and no one is feeding us?

What if animals know they are sacrificing their physical lives when they become prey to other, hungry animals?

The hunters who guided me on safari in Africa told me they believed that the animal who is prey instructs his or her soul to leave the body just as the painful attack by a predator occurs. Animals know that the laws of survival are in effect, and some kind of animal karma is enacted. They also said that the same thing occurs in the case of human hunters who need to eat animals in order to survive. The animals sacrifice their physical lives for the sake of the human who needs food. Their souls go on living.

Animal experts have explained to me that animal souls tend to be more collective than individualistic. They relate to their collective species more than to themselves—hence, pack behavior, herds, flocks, etc.

The first time I went to Africa, I thought I had joined a photographic safari. No, my mistake. It was a hunting safari. I found myself more concerned for the well-being of the animals than for the safety of the humans. On my last day, the hunting party came across a magnificent mother black panther and her cubs lounging in a tree. Black panthers are considered royal game in Africa, which means humans were not allowed to hunt them. The people I was with were ready to violate that restriction, and I couldn't take it. I took a rifle from a knapsack and trained it on my hunting group, threatening to kill them if they harmed the panthers in any way. I was dropped from the group and ushered back to a makeshift hut to wait for a small plane to pick me up.

I think of those panthers so often. I was told they were relocated to safety after I left, but how can they ever be safe from humans who only want trophies?

What if something happens to my dog Terry?

I would get another dog immediately, and wait for Terry to come back. I believe the life she has led has been too pleasurable for her to ignore.

Until then—because I can't bear the thought of coming home to a house without Terry—I've now adopted a younger brother for her. *She found him.* I had tried a new baby dog a year prior, but it didn't work out. He was too young, and I was too old to chase after a six-week-old.

About a year later, I got the strongest feeling I should call the Malibu Pet Hospital, a place Terry was familiar with. Something—was it really Terry?—seemed to be telling me that I'd find a year-old male rat terrier (same kind of dog as Terry) there whom she could not only tolerate, but whom she would like to have around because he would add years to her life.

Long story short, there was indeed a boy rat terrier named Buddy, whose human father had not returned to retrieve him. He needed a home, and I thought he needed a big sister/mom. Terry adored him immediately—of course she did; adopting him had been her idea. I call him Buddy-Bub. They play and pummel and roll around and jump on each other. It is a joy to watch them—a 108-year-old lady (in human years) cougaring an 8-year-old youngster. A little extreme, but adorable. They'll be lifelong pals until Terry decides to move on, and I hope she will come back right away. She will let me know, and I will hear her in my head again. Thanks to Terry, I have learned I can love more than one soul equally.

They are my most precious entertainment. As long as there are dogs in the world, I will be happy.

What if people were more like dogs?

People often tell me that the passing of their beloved dog was more devastating than the passing of a relative.

Why?

A dog will always tell you the truth, no matter what. No studio head could succeed in "improving" a doggie's life script.

What if Terry and Buddy-Bub decide to *pre*-incarnate?

Perhaps they know how devastated I will be when they pass, so maybe they will *pre*-incarnate in other puppies, which I will recognize. Will they be living two lives at once? All time is happening at once anyway, so why not?? That's what I call Mortality Wisdom, not science fiction.

What if we simply need to ask the right questions instead of trying to find all the right answers?

I try to think of answers as springboards to more questions.

What if we understood and harnessed the greatest creative forces of life? Our souls.

What if Show Business is a form of shamanism?

What if Dean Martin and Jerry Lewis hadn't broken up?

One of Hollywood's most famous comic performers would have been murdered, a crime that Dean would have readily confessed to committing.

The day they broke up, Jerry was outlining a scene in a movie he was writing. A comical crime had been committed, and Jerry had his character and Dean's pursuing the police at high speeds. Dean objected. Jerry asked why. Dean said, "Because the only times I was ever in a chase with the cops, they were in my rearview mirror . . . not the other way around."

Jerry said that didn't fit what he was writing. Dean got up and said, "Then I don't fit, either." He left, slamming the door, and they didn't see each other again for over twenty years. I heard about this because their agent, who was also my agent, was in the room when it happened.

I've often wondered how the dynamics of almost any duo can be sustained over time. Perhaps polar opposites are not made to last long into the future. They smolder and combust in the present.

Years later, Frank Sinatra surprised Jerry by bringing him and Dean back together again for a charity fund-raiser. It was a telethon, and Jerry was the host. Dean walked back through the door he had walked out of two decades earlier. Out of sheer force of habit, they launched right into a comedy routine as though they had never been apart. This particular dynamic of polar opposites was pure combustible joy for one more night.

Frank was a good one for putting people together. Maybe if he had been in the room, they never would have split. But, then, "if a frog had wings . . ." Some what-ifs aren't worth contemplating.

What if synchronicity were available to us every moment?

I think it is. Here's a recent example from my own life.

For a week and a half I had been thinking about a moment from early in my career, sixty years ago in fact, and I was trying to make sense of it. I was dancing in a show in a regional theater-in-the-round in Lambertville, New Jersey. The theater was called St. John Terrell's Music Circus. We performed a different Broadway show every week. I was eighteen years old and had just graduated from high school. The summer season came to an end, and I was anxious to get back to Manhattan quickly. One of the backstage laborers had a pickup truck and was driving toward the city. I didn't know him at all; maybe he wasn't even officially attached to the show. Still, I asked him if I could hitch a ride with him. "Sure," he said.

My question now, all these years later, was: Why did I get into a truck with a strange man for what must have been a two-hour ride? The question haunted me for a week and a half, I couldn't shake it.

On the last day of puzzling over this small detail, I went to a dancing event in L.A. where I was being honored. At the dinner afterward, a woman approached me at my table. With trepidation, she leaned over and said, "Hello, I'm Roberta Silbert, and I've been wanting to talk to you for years about something you and I did one summer in Lambertville, New Jersey."

I couldn't believe what I was hearing.

"You probably don't remember anything about that summer, it must have been sixty years ago," she continued, "but I was your understudy for the summer season at St. John Terrell's Music Circus."

"Another understudy story," I thought, "relating to my life!"

"After the last show, you and I hitched a ride to New York with some guy we hardly knew. I've always wondered why we did that. And now, after following your life for sixty years, I'm right here with you and can ask you the question directly. Why did we feel all right about getting in that truck with some big, strapping guy we didn't know from Adam?"

I couldn't speak. It was so perfectly synchronistic. I told

her I had been thinking about that very night for the last week and a half and needed an answer to that question myself. I hadn't remembered that she had been with me until she said so. I was initially so stunned by her bringing up Lambertville, New Jersey, out of the blue, sixty years after the fact, that for a split second I thought it was some sort of hoax. But then she mentioned numerous details of the summer that assured me she was completely authentic.

Suddenly I realized that the reason we got into the truck was because we knew we could depend on each other in a bad situation. We were both athletic and in good shape and had spent the summer dancing in stock together, which is a bonding experience. Surely that was why we felt comfortable getting into that truck.

The universe had provided me with the answer to my question, but now I wanted to know *why*. Why had this part of my past come back into my consciousness at precisely the same time I was about to meet the only person on the planet who could help me understand it? What was I supposed to see or learn besides recognizing the incredible power of synchronicity yet another time?

The woman and I exchanged numbers, and I began to ponder the bigger question. Maybe there's a lesson there about female friendships, or about taking risks, or about the nature of the understudy/leading lady relationship. But the main lesson I took to heart from this unexpected encounter? Friendships always return, and timing is everything!

What if the Hollywood studio system were still intact?

I love to remember it. They tell me that I was the last of the contract players. I had what was called in Hollywood slang a "white slave" contract, with producer Hal B. Wallis at Paramount Studios. It was a five-year contract, but after being slapped with several suspensions because I didn't like the scripts, I saw my contract extended to seven years. I sued him and won my freedom from that contract. That was the end of my being a part of the studio system, and with my victory, a precedent had been set—the end of the entire contract player studio system was inevitable. Later I'd wonder, had I won the battle and lost the war?

What a glorious time it was in some ways, though. Of course I was in trouble if I refused a script Wallis and Paramount ordered me to do. But the studio environment lingers in my memory like a banquet of famous faces—brilliant writers, astute producers, controlling studio heads, and the people who, everyone understood, were really in control of it all: the directors. My first studio dressing room was on the Paramount lot. It was a little bungalow, one in a long row of bungalows assigned to other actors. My next-door neighbor on one side was Anna Magnani, who had just won an Oscar for *The Rose Tattoo,* and on the other side was Lizabeth Scott, who supposedly was Hal Wallis's mistress. She was nice, though, and quiet, and seemed to appreciate having a place on the stars' row. The rest of the row housed Dean Martin, Jerry Lewis, Danny Kaye, Elvis Presley, Burt Lancaster, and Shirley Booth.

There was a fish pond in the center of the garden back then, and we actors would gather around it, talking about our careers, the scripts we were expected to do, and life in Hollywood. Jerry Lewis was the cutup, of course, but Dean was the truly funny one. The supremely handsome Burt had a tendency to stride around or silently lurk, which intrigued me for some reason. But I couldn't ever really figure him out because he never spoke a word.

Zsa Zsa Gabor would often flit by, stopping just for a moment to talk about jewelry with me.

Danny Kaye rode around on his bicycle, just being supremely talented. Little did I know then that I would have a love affair with him twenty-five years later, which proved to me that he was not gay—at least not completely. He flew me to various cities around the globe for exquisite dinners; he was an accomplished pilot and chef. I ended our love affair the day I realized his face reminded me of my mother's!

That's the thing about aging. The past comes to seem like a piece of theater I was scarcely in. I remember it more as an observer than a participant. The world and everything in it seemed so different then. This feeling of disconnect produces a shift in "space-time" consciousness for me. Was the past *I* experienced real? How much of it has been rewritten by the passing of time and my own desire to recall it in a certain way? When you tell a good story enough times, it becomes far more real than any so-called truth.

There were no freeways when I first came to Hollywood. Now when I travel them, I'm constantly reminded of the sweetness of the past—the slow pace, the depth of a single moment, my limited understanding of how the world worked. I think of the people I had around me and how safe they made me feel. Ignorance really was bliss then. I didn't know enough to be concerned about anything. Life was a fabulous entertainment.

I remember the mornings I walked into the hair and makeup department at Metro, where I shot *Some Came Running, Two Loves,* and several other pictures. Memory is so selective and tricky, but there, stretched across the forty-foot-long mirror, sitting quietly in chairs waiting for Sydney Guilaroff to tend to their hairdos, were Jean Simmons, Audrey Hepburn, Grace Kelly, Kathryn Crosby (in full makeup and color-coordinated outfit), Elizabeth Taylor, Susan Hayward, and Debbie Reynolds. I sat down in my designated chair and made a conscious decision to remember every detail of that morning. I'm so glad I did, because in just a few years, most people wouldn't remember half the talented people working in the studio, or even be acquainted with the glory days of the Hollywood studio system. It was all taken for granted then, and even seemed somewhat mundane to those of us who worked within it.

The celebrity culture was not to hit for another fifty years. We were isolated, protected, paparazzi-free, and relatively unbothered. Our surroundings were perfect and paid for.

The studio commissaries were cotillions for gossip and interchange. The press was often there at lunch, stopping by tables, picking up stories, watching deals being made. But when I look back and try to grasp a specific memory, to zero in on my *personal* experience, what comes to mind is how much butter I would slather onto the matzos and whether my stomach would protrude at an after-lunch fitting! Memory is different from in-the-moment experience. Today I regret not having been more consciously aware of the magical kingdom I was so intimately a part of.

I wonder now what became of the massage master I went to every day on the lot, certain that deep massage would curtail my hip fat. Where is Edith Head, whom I stood so obediently in front of, knowing she would accentuate my favorable parts and disguise the ones I hated? Studio heads were intimidated by her because they knew she had the power to make their stars (male and female) happy or not. If Edith wanted to, she could cause an insecure actress to have a violent temper tantrum after seeing her dailies.

Where is Nellie Manley now, who was head of the makeup department at Paramount? She boasted of her relationship with Marlene Dietrich, who she claimed ate only every three days; that was how she kept her streamlined figure. I remember sitting in on one of Marlene's fittings for a rhinestone-studded dress. It lasted three hours because Marlene insisted on moving around the rhinestones to achieve the desired effect. I think Marlene taught Orry-Kelly (the famous costume designer) to sew 10.5-millimeter pearls into the nipple area of the particularly tight dresses he created.

Fittings were of paramount importance to us actresses, because we all knew that the camera puts ten pounds on the body. I was luckier than most, because I am big-boned and therefore looked slimmer on camera than I actually was. Not anymore. But now I don't care so much. I'd rather be happy.

And happy I was in the studio system, even though I and everyone else always complained about scripts and money and loan-outs. When a studio owned you, it had the right to loan you out to any other studio for whatever it could charge. We contract players were paid what our contracts stated. I, for example, was loaned out once for $750,000 and was paid $6,000, per my contract. Worth a complaint or two, I thought.

However, the studios became our family environment

because we spent more time there than at home. Whenever I worked with Dean and Frank together, the lunches in their dressing rooms were old-world classic. The food would come from high-priced Italian restaurants with antipasto fit for royalty, probably delivered by whatever Mob guy was in town. The Mob was prevalent in their lives because the Mob owned all the saloons the singers sang in. Relationships were established, and the Mob guys were entranced by the singers' talent and fame, and the singers were thrilled by the proximity to danger, by the drama and mystery of how the Mob operated, and fascinated at the way they did what they did for a living without any pangs of conscience.

I was so young that none of it fazed me. The "boys" and the singers were fun to be around, and they treated me as a talented mascot who cleaned up their mess after lunch or dinner. I always found it interesting that none of them ever asked about my personal life. They knew I was married, but they never met my husband. They never made a move on me, and they never asked me any questions. My husband was away much of the time, working in Asia, but that was my business, no one else's. When the Rat Pack was together, I was theirs. They protected me, and that was that. Years later, I heard that there had been some talk of kidnapping my daughter for ransom, but Frank put an end to that, and whenever anything in my life went wrong, he'd call and ask how he could help.

Of course, the studio heads were wary of Frank's moods and opinions. His fame, talent, and associates were intimidating. He didn't shrink from using his assets! But Dean was more of the real McCoy, Mob-wise. He used to deal blackjack at the tables owned by the Mob. In fact, he was in the pit dealing the night Bugsy Siegel opened the Flamingo. I watched the studio heads evaluate Dean after the breakup with Jerry, and *before* his collaboration with Frank. They weren't sure what to do with Dean. Was he handsome? Was he funny? Was he just a singer? Could he act? It wasn't until *Some Came Running* that he found his identity—a funny singer who could always get the girl and knew where the bodies were buried. His agent was my agent, so we always knew what each other was up to. I had a crush on Dean for an hour or two, but nothing ever came of it because his wife, Jeannie, was always there and I liked her just as much.

As I reflect on my studio days with no small amount of nostalgia, I find myself longing to understand who we thought we were and what we thought we were doing. We were involved with each other's lives as though the real world were an outside entity. That's when we started calling people who weren't in show business "civilians." We were naïvely arrogant about our roles in life, believing that nothing could harm us and that as long as we were pretty good on the screen, we'd be "adored" in real life. The sun was always shining, the limos were instantly available, the publicity departments sculpted our images, the wardrobe departments made our clothes and gave them to us afterward if we wanted them, the catering tables were stocked with goodies, and we could sleep around if we wanted to without fear of consequence or judgment.

There were lavish dinners and parties every weekend, peopled by famous faces dressed in the latest styles and adornments. The main course and dessert were usually flambé, served tableside, masterfully handled by gloved attendants who also made sure the white wine was poured just as the fish course was about to be served. There were tennis lunches and trips to Palm Springs, where deals were brokered and the second homes of the rich and famous were opened up for weekend house parties.

Sometimes we'd all pile onto a train bound for Las Vegas. Gin rummy was played for a thousand dollars a point, and when we got to Vegas we were comped for the entire weekend. They were glad to have us because we inspired gambling. Drinks were free, as were all the meals—the finest cuisine in the world. There were no clocks in the casinos, and the indoor temperature was kept consistently cool. (The better for gambling; you never wanted gamblers to sweat!)

I never knew who was sleeping with whom. It somehow didn't interest me. And no one—no producer, no studio head—ever propositioned me, either. In fact, in all my years in the studio system, I wasn't even aware of the casting couch. I basically had a dancer's mentality: work hard, be disciplined, be a team player, don't cause trouble, be cooperative, and show up on time. With that value system, I guess I wasn't fodder for propositions. That didn't mean, though, that I didn't fall in love with my costars. I did. With almost every single one of them.

We were famous, rich, protected, fun-loving human actors in a magical tale of comedy, drama, romance—all set in a phantasmagorically closed world. Beverly Hills was our "gritty" downtown, and Malibu our trek into rough-and-ready nature. But who were we? The closed bubble of it all is what drove me to travel and explore the world. I knew somehow that it wasn't healthy or real, even though everyone else seemed to dream of living exactly the way we did.

I began to become aware that there were indeed other, different realities being served up by life. My famous face was a passport to any country I wanted to visit, and I found that I was readily accepted into wildly different situations and circumstances all over the world. The traveling, then, became an education in "otherness" for me. There was so much that I wasn't aware of.

I don't know why I knew I had to go. I had to travel. I had to learn. I had to know. I had to say "what if." The unreal studio system forced me into the real world.

But now with the reflection that comes with age, I have to say, I miss it. If the studio system had prevailed, perhaps the studios themselves could have avoided being bought by corporations. It is corporate thinking that has necessitated filmmakers' devoting their time and creativity to "branded" blockbusters. Because now Hollywood's studio system is all about money and special effects, not the cinematic art of capturing human life. That task now belongs to the independent filmmakers, and in the current shrinking economy, it is extremely difficult to get financing.

In the old days the studio heads would more often than not throw up their hands and go along with the crazy artists, the writers, directors, actors—the visionaries. This in turn satisfied their secret desire to be "artists" in show business, too, rather than businessmen and numbers guys in suits. It worked. When they rubbed shoulders with these artists and performers, they knew for sure that they were not in some assembly-line business making cars or toothpaste.

Now, with corporate ownership, the studio heads are in the assembly-line business of making brands. It's all about profit and loss, not visionary cinematic communication anymore. Yes, I miss the old days, but then, I wish there were no freeways, either. I like the side streets, the ones where you don't always know what's around the next curve, where you drive at a more leisurely pace and take in the view, without the rush for the final destination—without keeping your eye only on miles covered or gasoline burned.

What if I broke out of the Hollywood star system because I insisted on being psychically honest?

What if I had a stalker?

I think I have been lucky in so many respects. The paparazzi have never made my life miserable, and apparently I'm not the personality type that crazy people obsess over.

I've always felt that being open, even to a fault, eliminates the mystery that attracts obsession. What more can the stalkers or press find out about me that I haven't already shared? When you believe in reincarnation and extraterrestrials, and you say so, there's not a lot for anyone to stalk or pursue.

So my secret to being allowed to go about my business is: "Don't conceal—Reveal."

What if people stopped repeating themselves? There would be a lot of unused air and still practically no communication.

What if we are coming to resemble our own technology?

Are we thinking and communicating with the speed of the Internet—and ignoring the depth and breadth of what we actually feel? We can get any fact in a nanosecond, but getting wisdom still takes a lifetime (or more!).

Do our leaders mask evil intentions with glorious rhetoric?

That's just an old show business trick. One that still works.

What if Lucifer had the starring role in the first act of *Freewill Democracy*?

Lucifer was supposed to have been the most enlightened of the angels—hence his name (meaning "Angel of Light"). And if anyone was a candidate for freewill democracy, it was the enlightened one. And he made the choice to part ways with God and call his own shots.

But once you part company with God (the ultimate director), perhaps you become "crazy" (a diva?), because you now have no connection with the all-encompassing, over-whelmingness of *true* reality (God). Therefore, you suffer from the dis-easement of perceiving only limited Reality (physical life). What if the truth is that we have each had many lifetimes (roles) and have each been many people on many other worlds (location living). Without maintaining the fundamental connection to the Creator, we couldn't possibly know who we are, because the Creator is the Informer.

Perhaps we have simply followed the footsteps of Lucifer in defiance of Divine Law and we are reaping the rewards of living in a state of limited reality: Insanity (aka a film set).

Since more than six billion people live on this planet, and democracy means that we get to use our free will as the means of setting the goals for mankind, perhaps this planet is ungovernable and, in effect, *CRAZY*. Democracy, with all its diverse points of view, represents a populace that seems to be ungovernable. We are destroying ourselves, our earth home, our future, in the name of our freedom *because* we live in a democracy. What if democracy is a trick perpetrated on the human race by higher-level beings who want to control us in the guise of freedom of choice? We can't decide what we want, so we can't choose in our best interest. I'm certain this script has been financed and has a distributor! (Global elite? Illuminati? Etc., etc.)

Democracy is having a hard time because we don't understand the consequences of our individual freedoms and choices. We are free to be profitably materialistic (in the short term) at the expense of destroying Nature and life itself.

Could this be the human script? The first act is about our Founding Fathers, who wrote the road map and the rules for this system of government. Many of them belonged to the Masonic order. We flashback to what it meant to be a

Mason. Why was the Masonic order shrouded in secrecy for so long? (Maybe the wardrobe was difficult to wear.)

To digress for a moment: my grandfather (mother's dad) was a thirty-three-degree Mason in Canada. I never knew that until, upon Mother's death, I found papers and newspaper articles that praised his intelligence (he was a brain surgeon) and mentioned his involvement with a Masonic order.

[Fade in: exposition relating the story line told in Voice Over.] The Masonic order is a relatively secret *world* organization that believes we are not alone in the universe and that reveres the bloodlines of the ancients down through time. The organization's worldwide secrecy, which seems to bind its members together, comes as a result of having suffered through much of history at the hands of the Catholic Church, and many Masons were executed during the Inquisition. Friday the thirteenth is considered unlucky because that was the day the Knights Templar (part of the Masonic order) were rounded up by the Catholic hierarchy and executed. Hence, the need for secrecy. Fourteen of our presidents were Masons who freely believed in reincarnation (the physical reembodiment of the soul through time in order to learn). [End of Voice Over.]

The second act begins with a question: Were we meant to have a spiritual democracy in the United States? Perhaps Masonic members were the forerunners to the establishment of one world spiritual government and a one world currency because they were in possession of cosmic wisdom regarding life beyond earth. The Masonic order believes deeply in the power of sacred geometry. That is why the Masonic apron depicts the compass and the square. Perhaps the cosmos itself is a sacred geometric design that is like a Grand Book full of all truth, and our task is to learn the language with which to read it.

The third act has not been written yet . . . it is too complicated to imagine the story as of now!

What if our Congress were enlightened enough to understand that separation of church and state (religion and government) is the forerunner to a Spiritually Enlightened democracy?

What if many of our nation's Founding Fathers openly shared with each other their belief in extraterrestrial life? What if an extraterrestrial presence revealed to them a Divine Plan for the United States of America that served as their guide and inspiration?

I'd say there is no "what if" about this.

George Washington, Thomas Jefferson, Benjamin Franklin, John Adams, Thomas Paine, and the lesser known Benjamin Banneker openly and seriously discussed "the plurality of worlds" because each one of them had had a direct experience with what they believed was extraterrestrial life.

Jefferson, at the time he was vice president, was also president of the American Philosophical Society. He reported to the Society that "on the night of April 5, 1800, in Baton

Rouge, Louisiana, [naturalist William Dunbar] observed a large, glowing object about 70 or 80 feet long 200 yards above the surface of the Earth." It was luminous, shot out sparks, and appeared directly over the heads of many spectators, emitting a considerable degree of heat. Immediately after it disappeared in the skies to the northeast, a violent rushing noise was heard as if it had crashed. Jefferson said, "I've been informed a search was made where the burning body fell. A considerable portion of the earth was found broken up. Every vegetable body was burned and scorched."

There are remarkable accounts in the Library of Congress of George Washington's experiences at Valley Forge. While the army was camped there, he used to go alone into a forest thicket and pray for guidance. He often discussed the "visions" he had during these times. He said he saw "green-skinned men" in the forest with whom he communicated. Something happened to him at Valley Forge that inspired him and turned the tide of the Revolutionary War. He claimed to have been sitting in his cabin at Valley Forge when a luminous angel appeared to him and in a picture formed "on a cloud of vapor" revealed to him the future of the United States. His friend Anthony Sherman wrote that General Washington told him he saw a brilliant angel who showed him a panorama of what the United States would become. He said he felt strange emotions spreading through him, "a new mysterious influence, potent and irresistible, took possession of me." The surrounding atmosphere was luminous. Then he heard a voice repeat many times, "Son of the Republic, look and learn. Remember we are brethren." Sherman wrote an article about this for the *National Tribune,* but it wasn't printed until almost a century later.

The angel showed Washington much conflict in the new Republic but at the end declared, "While the stars remain and the heavens send down dew upon the earth, so shall the Union last. Let every child of the Republic learn to live for his God, his land and the Union." Washington said to Sherman, "With these words the angelic being vanished and I felt I had seen of the birth, progress and destiny of the United States."

Benjamin Franklin was seemingly more interested in "superior beings on the plurality of worlds" than any of his fellow Founding Fathers. In *Poor Richard's Almanack,* September 1749, he wrote: "It may be the opinion of all modern philosophers and mathematicians that the planets are habitable worlds." He was obsessed with looking at the stars and speculating on extraterrestrial life. In a letter to a friend he wrote, "Superior beings smile at our theories and at our presumptions in making them."

The Founding Fathers often discussed whether intelligence from above (and not only that of the Divine) was inflaming the genius that led to the creation of the Declaration of Independence and the US Constitution.

The Founding Fathers were very familiar with Native Americans' legends and their knowledge of the Star People. They spoke of glowing individuals who came down in "flying baskets" and took men and women as star-wives and star-husbands. Later, much of our Constitution was based on the laws and structure of the Iroquois Confederacy, a longtime union of Native American tribes.

Thomas Paine included a long description of other solar systems in *Age of Reason,* which spread other worldly ideas far beyond the realm of intellectuals. Paine felt the idea of other planetary habitation was incompatible with Christianity and was evidence against religion.

John Adams, second president of the United States, made the following entry in his diary on April 24, 1756: "All the unnumbered worlds that revolve around the fixt stars are inhabited, as well as this Globe of Earth."

The Lunar Society, a very popular organization in the Revolutionary era, became the hub for discussions of the plurality of worlds among the Americans and the French. Bernard le Bovier de Fontenelle, a French intellectual and author, wrote *Conversations on the Plurality of Worlds,* the book that Jefferson and Franklin used as their resource and guide. It was translated into English in 1687. It is written as a kind of dialogue while observing the stars.

But it was Benjamin Banneker, a free black man and intellectual, who inspired the Founding Fathers to consider seriously the plurality of worlds. He said he had come from the Dogon tribe in Africa, which we know mysteriously possessed advanced and accurate knowledge of astronomy and star systems hundreds of years ago. Banneker was extremely close to Jefferson and Franklin and influenced them greatly regarding their ideas about other worlds and the superior beings who resided there.

In his book *Articles of Belief and Acts of Religion,* Franklin wrote, "I believe there is one Supreme most perfect Being, Author and Father of the Gods themselves. For I believe that man is not the most perfect Being but One, rather that as there are many Degrees of Beings his inferiors, so there are many Degrees of Beings superior to him." Franklin also wondered if there was a God for every inhabited planet.

The city of Washington, DC, was laid out to acknowledge a unique celestial connection. According to many scholars, the nation's capital has been steeped in ancient symbolism since its inception. Ancient astronaut theorists point to the city's tallest structure, the Washington Monument, as proof that the American capital was built with a deliberate eye to the stars. Although construction began in 1848, more than fifty years after George Washington's death, the Freemasons built the Egyptian-style monument so the constellation Pleiades would be visible directly over the giant obelisk. The Pleiades are a group of seven bright stars, which ancient Egyptians used as an aid in making judgments. In the ancient world, in places of great power and great influence, they built monuments aligned with this constellation. The Washington Monument is aligned with the Pleiades on December 3 at night or July 4 during the day. Some say the alignment occurs at the winter solstice.

Some historians believe the triangle of important monuments found in the middle of Washington, DC, represents the square and compass, symbolizing the Founding Fathers' search for enlightenment from above. Ancient astronaut theorists claim beyond this triangle lies an even more significant shape, that of a pentagram. George Washington and Thomas Jefferson were both expert surveyors and mapmakers, and were hands-on in the design of Washington, DC. Some speculate Washington and Jefferson built this starlike design in case of an extraterrestrial visitation, in hopes the image would be recognized and symbolize our respect for extraterrestrial life.

The primary triangle, connecting the Capitol building and the White House to the Washington Monument, was key. Some scholars believe that the triangle found in the city represents the Masonic square and compass, symbolizing the Founding Fathers' search for enlightenment from above.

The interesting thing about Jefferson's influence on the design of Washington, DC, was this pentagram, with roads emanating in every direction from it so that it seems to be a mirror of the heavens. Jefferson did believe that the heavens were inhabited and wanted Washington, DC, not just to be the capital of the United States of America, but the capital of the universe.

The Capitol Rotunda is literally a vortex of energy. Domes are places where heaven and earth meet. They are considered to be portals, or gateways, to the stars.

In 1791, architect Pierre L'Enfant declared Washington, DC's Jenkins Hill a "pedestal waiting for a monument." For the next two years he worked closely with Washington and

Jefferson to design the building that would sit atop this hill and be the home of the US Congress. On September 18, 1793, the day of the autumn equinox, Washington laid the cornerstone for the Capitol building and Jenkins Hill became Capitol Hill, the heart of a new democracy. The concept of the ancient and sacred hill was etched deeply in the minds of the Founding Fathers: even Jefferson's beloved Monticello was built atop a mound. But was the design and placement of the Capitol really influenced by alien beings? Ancient astronaut theorists point to evidence in the form of a statue that still sits atop the Capitol dome, the Freedom Statue. It was placed there after the dome was completed in 1866. It's a nineteen-foot-tall statue of a goddess who is actually morphing into an eagle. In ancient alien theory, alien gods were portrayed as "eagle-headed." Is freedom being referenced here as a star being?

I believe I had a past lifetime during the American Revolution when I lived as Robert Morris. Morris was a wealthy merchant who personally financed a great deal of the revolution and oversaw the health of the infant US economy, yet he spent time in prison and died penniless because of failed land speculations. I, therefore, am careful with money, refuse shady deals, and am possessed of a patriotism that feels almost mystical about being an American.

If my research in this area should come to be accepted as fact, then our revolution will come to be seen as having been divinely inspired, and there will be no more "what if" about it!

What if elections focused less on manipulating the negative and more on the emergence of positive new ideas—ideas that are not already society-accepted homilies?

What if Obama stepped back into playing only the role of president of the United States?

I have a theory. I think he'd enjoy being president of the planet. I was struck by how comfortable in his skin he seemed during the first campaign when speaking to the throngs gathered at the Brandenburg Gate; and equally comfortable speaking in front of thousands of Muslims in Cairo; and again while apologizing to the intellectuals of Europe for America's past actions. He seems to see himself as a human leader who is familiar with all races, creeds, and points of view. After all, he *is* white, black, Christian, Muslim, sharp, dull, and male (yang) with a strong dash of female (yin). He seems to want to fight for the human, not just the American, underdog. So *who is he*? Is he too much of everyone to be anyone? A dash of everything that leaves no strongly identifying flavor?

Perhaps he is an amalgamation of everything that makes up America, which allows us to excoriate him on levels we don't understand and aren't aware of in ourselves.

But what if his dream is to create one unified world order? Would Obama be a good planetary president? He can play all the parts—and he has.

What if the Dalai Lama were a news junkie? Would he be as sanguine as he is, seemingly without stress and judgment?

He says he doesn't keep up with any earth-plane events. Doesn't watch television or movies and is unaware of the news. Perhaps that is the most useful advice for all-around good health that there is. The news is show business disguised as information. Like everything else on television, it is all about the ratings. If war didn't get ratings, there wouldn't be any.

According to the Dalai Lama, none of it matters anyway. He says he is secure in his inner peace. I'm sure he is. The two weeks I spent with him in Rio de Janeiro, at the World Peace Conference in 1992, were very revealing. He spoke in front of crowds of twenty-five thousand people and never had a note in front of him for reference. His script came from somewhere above. Somehow he always managed to speak on a subject the collective mind wanted to hear. He was funny, profound, and seemed way ahead of the twenty-five thousand people in front of him, who presumably kept up with current events.

Every now and then, out of the blue, he would begin to laugh; no one knew why or at what! He laughed with one astonished crowd for about ten minutes, never explained the reason, and never apologized. Soon the crowd began to laugh, too. Twenty-five thousand people left that event happier than when they came in. Maybe that was the point. And the audience didn't have to pay; he did it for free.

Once, in Los Angeles, he spoke before an extremely sophisticated crowd: movie stars, business executives, studio heads, press pundits, etc. We expected a treatise on the way to achieve peace in the world. Instead, he did an hour on the profundity of a smile. I'll never forget one thing he said that night: "In traffic," he said, "you should lean over and smile at the car next to you." The right message for the right city!

I found him to be a bit of a flirt. He would find me in the audience (usually up front) and send me a wink and a smile. Once, as I was coming out of a ladies' room, he took my hand, which was still damp from washing. "Very nice," he said, laughing. For once in my life, I was at a loss for words!

Later I saw a clip on YouTube where he was asked to

discuss the conflicts inherent in differing religions, phi-
losophies, and political points of view. He raised his hand,
leaned forward, and said two simple words: "Fuck it." I
play that YouTube clip whenever I'm worried that I ask too
many questions about things other people take for granted.
If those two words are good enough for the Dalai Lama,
they are good enough for me.

What if there are incomplete dimensions to our Constitution? Is it meant to be a spiritual document as well as a political one?

What if Spiritual democracy is the answer? Where do Lucifer and hell fit within it?

What if we really grasped the profound *theatricality* of the so-called theater of war?

First of all, the cast of soldiers is all dressed up—they carry their military props and strut about on their preparatory stages with guns and explosives. They've rehearsed long and hard. They assure themselves that their bodies are lean and mean. And they wear their medals of reward proudly. They scream and yell violent warnings in lieu of dialogue, and usually go to battle with a marching band of some sort and are in perfect sync like well-trained chorus girls, kicking and stepping in unison.

They are instructed to think about dying as heroes so the audience will be with them, particularly if they die courageously. They will get the equivalent of their star on the

Hollywood Walk of Fame; their gravestone in the cemetery, which will be surrounded by well-kept scenery in a garden with well-watered flowers and fountains—like a movie heaven.

There is a casting problem, though. The theater-of-war soldiers only barely tolerate other cast members who are female. They don't appreciate costars in any case, but females? They detract from the killing process of the masculine warrior. Women costars should be behind the set, sewing costumes and polishing the brass.

The third act of the theater of military operations is a graveyard ceremony peopled by extras who feel patriotic as they stand silently to the musical strains of a twenty-one-gun salute. A marching band sends them off to kill. A musical fugue of earsplitting pounding sends them to heaven. The twist of this theatrical extravaganza (if reviewed properly) is that nobody actually kills anybody in the battle scenes of victory. Because nothing ever dies. The soldiers are actors performing what they rehearsed. They basically incur more karma for themselves because nobody asks, "What is this scene for? What's my motivation?" Or, more important, "Who do I have to boff to get out of this show?"

Show business is a teacher. It knows when a production is old-fashioned and needs a rewrite. Nobody should be asked to give their life for this show.

What if we promote the reasons for war because war (like show business) is a good investment? Has war become the hot new brand?

Holy Bible wars, religious freedom wars, tax wars, property wars, civil wars, terrorist wars, drug wars, first amendment wars and, last but not least, second amendment wars so that we have the firepower to fight all of the above.

If there are people who profit from war, it doesn't matter what issues are being fought over. The profit, not the cause or the resolution of the conflict, is the point.

What if patriotism, which we tend to think of as a virtue, becomes the motive for the crime? If killing is considered the highest cosmic and spiritual crime because it interrupts a soul's learning process, then it doesn't matter what we think we are protecting if it involves killing. It's particularly ironic, therefore, that so much killing in the theater of war is conducted in the name of God and "spiritual" values. How would you try a case like this? What is the law? The dramatic tension is served by two competing masters: the human judge and jury, and the God on whose book you swear to tell the truth and nothing but.

What if allowing political dissent is actually an effective tool for maintaining social and political control over a large population? Besides being economically profitable, fomenting conflict can be a way of securing and maintaining power. (A Malthusian script!) In a democracy, hearing opposing points of view gives us the reassuring feeling that we are free to express ourselves. But lurking in the background of this scenario is the possibility that stoking these opposing points of view can lead to the threat of violent conflict (which will always make money), which might in turn necessitate strong-armed control, which will give the military more jobs in a recession. The people go on squabbling with one another, totally unaware that their fighting actually benefits the military police, who "maintain the peace," and the ruling power, which maintains the police.

The democratic value of encouraging disagreement and embracing conflict via free expression can actually facilitate "crowd control." As that great director Machiavelli said, "Human disunity is a valuable commodity because it makes the people less able to mount a challenge to authority." At least in real show business you fight over "creative differences" and not whose God is better.

If everything were light, would there be any individuation?

What if violence and conflict served an important purpose?

Can we learn about ourselves without conflict? Can we learn about others without experiencing turmoil? Doesn't friction produce the fires of creativity? Life doesn't survive without creativity. If the flame of creativity comes from striking the match, does this mean God is a friction maker? Does God promote conflict because it is creative and self-revealing? What if all conflict exists because it enables us to see more of ourselves? What if life is simply a schoolroom of learning? In the final analysis, is the most important lesson knowing thyself? What else is there, really? What we see in others is only what we know exists in ourselves. So do we need conflict in order to find ourselves?

If violence and conflict are "musts" for popular entertainment, is entertainment their purpose, or, like the Roman
games, are they simply an effective diversion from the truth?
If we regarded all of life's experience as theater, perhaps we
wouldn't take it so seriously, therefore reducing the amount
of killing and full-blown war. Audiences may like being entertained by war, but they don't like participating in it.

The theaters of war and terror in the world are literally
financed by our fears. Fear makes money.

I believe our human purpose is to evolve to a higher level
of consciousness, to a more extended awareness of the multidimensional realities. Perhaps we need to learn about ourselves through conflict to do that. But we need to ask the
right questions. Otherwise this particular civilization may
run out of time. Haven't we already learned enough from
our violent experiences over the centuries?

To me, it is only logical to believe we all have lived many
lives, in many places. And I believe we are all star travelers.
That is why we are so interested in "space habitation." I believe we have all had experience living as star beings and we
continue to receive messages from celestial beings in multidimensional ways. To further that concept, what if there is
conflict among star nations and we humans and our wars
simply reflect that? As above, so below . . . Is all life everywhere an entertainment? A form of show business?

When I left Hollywood to travel the world (as I still
regularly do), I saw a deep longing and persistence in the

world for the greater spiritual and scientific truths. People everywhere are outgrowing traditional religion. They want to find their own truth and touch their own personal higher power. They want to know the truth about what lies beyond and among the stars. It's obvious to any thinking person that we are not alone, so why has there been a cover-up? People are making up their own minds about whether the disclosure of extraterrestrial life is a cause for panic or excitement. The New Age has come, and its priorities need to be respected.

The conflict comes as we decide what this will mean for the old, familiar ways of thinking that we must relinquish, and for the traditional power structures that will cease to have influence over us.

It's time to update the show.

What if we purposely managed to avoid bad people? Would we ever have the chance to learn anything about ourselves?

Bad people are more fun roles to act, but I don't think that means they are more fun to be.

What if we stopped the screening of airplane passengers right now—suddenly—all at once, and the thugs standing around (TSA) went home.

We wouldn't have to dress for disrobing—dis-shoeing, dis-hatting, dis-jacketing and dis-dogging. What if we were suddenly respected for being innately honest and peaceful without the need to prove we didn't shove anything up anywhere? What if my dogs, Terry and Buddy-Bub, could go to the gate without being felt up for an implanted bomb?

To date, the TSA has succeeded in apprehending with its pat-downs and machines:

Terrorist plots discovered	0
Transvestites	133

Hernias	1,485
Hemorrhoid cases	3,172
Incontinence cases	6,418
Enlarged prostates	8,249
Breast implants	59,350
Natural blondes	3

What if the incidence of cancer shot up because the TSA's machines were protecting us from death by terrorism, only to leave us with slow deaths from TSA-caused disease?

More important than any of the aforementioned, what if the "security" measures have never been predominantly about security, but more about the purposeful dumbing-down of Americans, making us subservient to control and authority? What if the point of amplifying fear is to render the population cooperative with its own individual captivity? Fear breeds handing over control, and handing over control breeds cooperative dumbing-down. In the name of protecting freedom and democracy, we've become prisoners of our own induced obedience.

What would we do now if all the invasive protection at airports were eliminated? Would we stand numbly by, waiting for someone in a uniform to come and search us in order to feel safe? Bring on *Hunger Games XIII*!

What if fear of terrorism becomes responsible for the creation of a third party—the Party of Citizen Oversight and Control, whose only mission would be to protect us from ourselves?

What if a state of war and terror is used to make populations change their sense of democratic freedom without their ever recognizing that it's happening? Can fear of terrorism make an entire population embrace values it would normally reject? Would a population even realize it was becoming more and more entrenched in and comfortable with institutions that ignore the Constitution in favor of the rule of law?

Just go to an airport and stand in line at the security checkpoint. Make people afraid enough, they will submit to anything.

What if anger is the motivator of change, particularly where homeland security is concerned?

A few times a month, I take the American Eagle flight from Santa Fe to L.A. and back again. I've been doing that since American Eagle installed that route. Before I got Buddy-Bub, I'd buy two seats in the bulkhead: a window seat for me and an aisle seat for my dog Terry in her bag. People loved to talk to her and pet her after asking permission, because she is a service dog. A service dog is accompanied by a doctor's certificate stating that the dog is necessary for the good health and safety of the owner, and my doctor says Terry is necessary to my sanity. (It sounds funny, but it's absolutely true!) I've made about fifty flights like this. The flight attendants and pilots have always been friendly and kind and professional.

The last flight I took with Terry, I experienced something different. There was a flight attendant who, before I even put Terry in her seat, began to order me around. "You can't sit there, and the dog has to be on the floor," etc. I fastened our seat belts and, remembering Alec Baldwin's ranting, which turned up all over the Internet and TV, kept my mouth shut. But the flight attendant wouldn't stop. Thinking she might be one of those who sometimes lose it and yell, "There's a bomb aboard!" I quietly said, "Why don't you call your manager?" Then I leaned up against the window and acted as though I'd fallen asleep.

The "manager" came and very sweetly said, "You have to sit in the aisle seat and put the dog on the window seat." I asked if I had to put Terry on the floor. He said no. I told him I'd had this seating arrangement for years and that nobody had ever objected. He said the flight attendant had looked it up in the Book and it said a service dog must sit by the window. I asked why. He smiled and said, "I don't know."

The flight attendant stepped up and yelled, "The rules are rules and these are the rules." I motioned for her to keep her voice down and asked why again. She said, "Rules are rules." The manager rolled his eyes.

I guess that's when I said, "Well, you'll have to remove me and Terry from the plane." He didn't know what to do. The flight attendant stood over us both. I didn't move. I knew I was digging myself in deeper, but the "rules" regarding homeland security were beginning to really bug me. The TSA agent at the security gate had already made a big deal out of swabbing my hands (for explosive residue, I guess) because I had a dog, and she had said, "There could be a bomb in her." I quietly said under my breath, "What if there's a bomb in you?" She didn't quite hear me, but she gave me a look like "You behave or there will be incarceration for you." I looked over and saw a man about ninety years old being felt up and down and in and out by a TSA thug. Tears were in his eyes.

My memory went to *The Reader*, with Kate Winslet playing the Nazi commandant who was "just obeying orders" as she sent people to the gas chamber. That character sincerely didn't believe she was doing anything morally questionable—just following the rules.

Now, as I sat in my seat on board the aircraft, I contemplated what I could do to illustrate how stupid all this was. I asked if I should sue the airline for not observing safety regulations all the other times I flew sitting by the window.

The answer: "Rules are rules."

"But why didn't they obey the rules before now?" I asked.

"Rules are rules." That's the answer you get, regardless of the circumstances.

The manager didn't know what to do with the flight attendant. I asked a barrage of questions, which is my proclivity, and wasted a lot of time. Even though the attendant was such a jerk, I didn't want the plane to be late taking off. I relented and sat in the aisle seat and moved Terry to the window. Then the attendant instructed us on exactly what we could and couldn't do during the flight. When the pilot spoke to us as we taxied to the runway, the crackling in his microphone was so pronounced we couldn't understand a single word. I thought, "Isn't that a violation of security?"

We arrived at our destination safely but not happily. I asked the name of the flight attendant. It was Crystal.

My God, I thought, it's crystal clear how ridiculously complicated the security machine has become. The passengers become the enemy, guilty until proven innocent, and the people in charge of our security just piss us off. Is that how the American Revolution was born? *People who became pissed off at being pissed on* . . . and by our very own "protectors." Maybe that's why we can't get gun control. People want to protect themselves against rules and control. There is a spiritual element to our political science missing somewhere.

What if a cynical attitude is a more realistic way of looking at the world than an optimistic attitude? What if it is the most healthy because it is the truest?

I like cynicism, because it provides humor in any culture. Without cynicism, there would be no comedy. There would be no revolutions. It bonds people, enabling them to force change. Cynicism exists as a warning to the status quo that it is failing. We laugh at a cynical remark because it pierces the heart of hypocrisy. For example, a friend of mine was asked if film school was a good education for a would-be director. He replied, "Not as good as two failed marriages and a stint in jail!"

We long to hear the truth. We can tolerate the truth

because cynical humor takes the edge off its devastating import.

But what if cynicism, by being entertaining, insulates us from the cruelty of the truth? I say always be aware of the rats who are setting up shop in the basement even as you do your best to recognize and appreciate all the good things around and above you.

What if Hope is a most dangerous emotion?

It is said that without Hope life is not possible. Countless celebrated books and films extoll Hope as a virtue. But what if Hope exists only as a struggling opposite to despair? By giving "Hope" such primacy, we give despair just as much power. To me, Hope would no longer be a necessary state of mind if we could relinquish despair. What if whatever it is that causes us despair is really only the basis of a hard and difficult lesson to learn?

What if Hope is a diversionary tactic we indulge in so as not to have to look at whatever has created the grounds for our despair in the first place? Hope can be tricky, even dangerous.

I don't acknowledge despair, therefore I stay away from

Hope. It is too defeatist. Hope allows us to relinquish our personal responsibility because it causes us to divert our attention from what we, on some level, are responsible for. Hope enables us to naïvely pursue a passive point of view with the belief that someone or something else will make things right. Hope is often used by defeatist individuals who don't take responsibility. To me, Hope is decidedly different from Prayer. Prayer denotes action and focus. You have to know what you want, what you need, in order to pray effectively. To me, Hope is passive wishing, while prayer is active focus with an emphasis on expecting that what you pray for will happen. I believe we should *know* what we want, not hope for it.

To me, prayer is talking to God (or to the "all that is"). Meditation is listening to the same force. That is the yin and yang of it all. Prayer is the yang (the outward expression); meditation is the yin (the inward receiving). Hope is the indecisiveness of both. No expression, no receiving. To me it is the diversion of progress and possibility. No wonder "Hope" is so popular. It requires no talent and not much thinking and *no* expression of the individual self.

Hope can be a trick. It absolves us of responsibility. It actually romanticizes despair. It serves the longing in us rather than the true possibilities. Instead of Opium we do Hopeium.

As Benjamin Franklin said, "He that lives upon hope will die fasting."

What if Mother Nature could perform for an audience?

Does anyone really believe that she doesn't? We certainly see her expressing herself with storms, earthquakes, tornadoes, drought, and global warming. Is she, as the Hopi shaman said, "a mother dog shaking off fleas"?

I would like to hear the specifics of what she teaches us with her magnificent "spectaculars." For example, are the colors of flowers vibrating at the same frequencies as the musical notes in the scale? Does all sound have color? I knew a woman who loved to attend symphony concerts just to "see" the colors the instruments were making.

What if drought is Mother Nature's way of teaching us

that we need to drink more water and yet we are polluting it everywhere?

What if falling snow is to remind us of the protection of white lights?

What if flooding occurs because it is time for us to wash our environments clean?

What if mud sticks to us because that is what we have become?

Maybe our unquenchable interest in dinosaurs is equal to our unquenchable thirst for oil? In their first time around, they were destroyed. In this second time around, they will destroy us.

What if the speed of Nature's show is accelerating in a way that is meant to beckon us humans to accelerate our consciousness? What if we are holding her back and that is why she is shaking us off?

What if the "violence" of Nature is simply her way of saying "hurry up" or you'll be left behind? Nature's violence is probably the most devastatingly dramatic and disturbing thriller to grace the screens of life—and we haven't even assigned it an X rating.

What if Nature is designed to be fuel efficient without man's help, but mankind, forgetting we are part of Nature, has tinkered with that design?

What if trees are silent actors communicating to us without words?

Why don't we hear them begging not to be cut down? Are they trying to tell us that by cutting them down we are diminishing our oxygen supply? Are they saying they will be our protectors in the future if we respect them now? Won't shade be even more necessary in the future as global warming speeds up?

When I lived in the Northwest, I once chased a crew of workers who had come to chop down a tree from my next-door neighbor's property. My neighbors were furious with me. I confess, I was not a good neighbor, but I was proud of myself and would gladly do it again today. And I suspect the audience would applaud.

What if all centers of corruption are being cleaned out with the violence of Nature?

What if this planet is going through a Big Flush?

What if our current chaos really is the beginning of Nature cleaning itself? What if we are at the beginning of a turnaround?

Perhaps, unknown even to ourselves, we are already operating at different frequencies than we used to, possessing a new and expanded consciousness. Maybe that's why the dark and the negative are so much more pronounced to us. We now *see* what we have to overcome. It is becoming clear. Is this Judgment Day? Is this the true Resurrection? Is this the Triumph of the Divine and the start of a thousand years of Peace?

I believe we will have the resurrection of the original divine blueprint of humanity throughout the cosmos, and mankind's degradation at the hands of the fallen gods will come to an end.

I believe there will be a colossal cleansing. Many will move on, and much will be "destroyed" in the cleansing process. But then I believe there will be vast armies of Divine Light Beings blocking the influence of the Dark consciousness. I believe the barriers between Life and the Divine Creator will fall so that there will no longer be a separation.

I believe we will finally understand our true origins and purpose as beings of light on the earth. I believe spiritual sciences and spiritual technologies will be the primary foundation for our education systems.

I believe it is time for the truth to be known about our origins. I believe it is time to recognize that we aren't now and never have been alone.

I believe it is time to understand that the history of this earth (and its inhabitants) has been a struggle against being the fearful victims of our past experiences. I believe that even though the entire cosmos is expanding and moving away from its parts, this widening separation will force us to look for the Divine Light within. After all, our interiors are as infinite as the exterior universe that is expanding. Let's move within ourselves and expand to infinity.

What if the grid goes down, either because of a natural phenomenon or an act of terrorism?

Imagine it. Communications are now nonexistent. No television, no radio. No weather warning systems. No telephone. No iPads, iPhones, or text messages. No transportation. We are each left with just ourselves and to our own devices. We are forced to make Nature our friend, the sort of friend we are loath to abuse or offend.

We live by the sun because there is no light after dark. We cook over homemade fires and have to draw water from a well by hand, unless it is gravity-fed. We have to devise our own entertainment at night because there is no electricity to bring us television, movies, or music from every corner of the globe.

Our hospitals come to a halt. Natural healing remedies are being practiced, and we've had to acquaint ourselves with the frequencies of homeopathic remedies. Surgery has become obsolete, and dental care makes do without X-rays or drilling. Grocery stores are without produce for a part of every year, because there is no gas flowing from the pumps to serve the trucks. Airplanes, trains, and ships can't operate without electricity, so the intimate knowledge of other countries' happenings and customs rapidly becomes minimal. The instantaneous global community soon becomes a thing of the past, and we come to understand that we are each on our own, responsible for our own survival.

If all this occurred, what would I be left with?

I'd have my garden to eat out of, my gravity-fed well for water, eggs from my chickens, heat and power from my solar panels, wind power from my windmills. I'd have the sun in the morning and the moon at night to remind me of my place in the cosmos. But more important than anything, I'd be forced into knowing myself better. Who am I and why am I here? I'd be part of Nature, not separated from her. I'd understand my animals more deeply. I'd listen to what children tell me with more patience. I'd witness the blooming of flowers with more wonder.

But mostly I'd need to grow into knowing what it means to be truly without distraction, without outside entertainment, and probably without a bank account. I'd have to learn to barter, which would elevate me into understanding the true priorities and value of "things."

I think I would become less self-centered, while understanding the centeredness of Self more.

What if it's necessary, then, for the grid to go down as a consequence of our not paying attention to the real values we have ignored for too long? This would be real natural entertainment. All show with no business.

What if our DNA is being activated into a new awareness?

Hopi and other Indian shamans believe there is a choice we have other than doom and gloom and death and destruction. They believe we are moving into a new land of being, a new frequency, a new dimension of existence. As we move through this process, they describe a variety of physical symptoms that humans are likely to feel.

I seem to be experiencing almost exactly what their list describes:

1. Headaches or nonlocalized pressure in the head;
2. Shifting or unstable vision;

3. Requiring one pair of glasses one day and a different pair the next;

4. A deepening sense of the ability to "see";

5. Sleep pattern interruptions;

6. Feelings that you are going crazy, losing your mind, or an inability to focus;

7. Emotional tenderness, mood swings, and "mania";

8. An embracing of unity consciousness;

9. Heightened sensitivity to smell, sound, and taste, or change in eating preferences;

10. Losing track of "time";

11. Physically dropping or bumping into things;

12. Hearing high-pitched tones or a series of tones or pressure in one or both ears;

13. Spiritual death or brief suicidal thoughts;

14. A heightened sense of not being in the present, or a sense of detachment;

15. A general sense of "free-flowing" energy that can often manifest and be misinterpreted as anxiety;

16. Jolts of energy that are felt physically and often will move the body;

17. Lack of focus and attention for any length of time;

18. Heightened, newfound discomfort with some public environments;

19. A sudden urge to make everything spacious, to release personal treasures, or to remove clutter from your environment;

20. Heartburn or chest pressure;

21. Attraction to new colors;

22. Change in priorities in your career/relationships; and

23. A feeling of time "moving fast."

What if California goes into the ocean?

I remember being in the audience watching the film *2012*. When Los Angeles slid into the Pacific, the crowd actually applauded! Were they saying, "Good riddance"? I saw *The Day after Tomorrow* in Santa Fe with a largely Hispanic audience. When Mexico closed its borders to the refugees from the United States escaping the ravages of an impending ice age, again everyone applauded and cheered. The shoes were on different feet.

Edgar Cayce predicted earthquakes and tsunamis that would devastate California. In fact, he saw the Eastern and Western Seaboards both going. He also saw the Mississippi River flowing backward and, in effect, America splitting into three countries: the remaining western and southwestern states, the Midwest, and what was left of the eastern states. Are the people of California intuiting these events, and is that why more people are moving out of the state than are moving in, for the first time ever?

The Golden State of Paradise is no longer the land of milk and honey. It is the land of economic uncertainty and of the New World "underwater"—financially and, maybe someday, literally.

What if my memory is going?

I don't think memory loss is altogether due to aging. In fact, I think "senior moments" are "memory not relevant moments." When you can't remember something, it's probably not relevant to the matter at hand anyway! Many young people I know are experiencing the same thing. Perhaps it is a result of the 2012 shift that was foreseen by the Mayans. To me, the Mayan calendar is a *consciousness calendar, not an event calendar,* with 2012 representing a moment when a shift in consciousness would occur, not the end of the world, as so many people thought.

Perhaps Nature, by making us increasingly forgetful, is saying, "You must begin to vibrate to the new frequency even if it means losing awareness of people and events you experienced before." Names, dates, and specifics from the past are no longer useful in a new vibration. Everything will change and become obsolete.

When I can't remember why or how I know someone, I try not to panic. I go into a deep breathing space that says, "It doesn't matter; they are having the same problem, or will soon!" I go immediately to the closest tree or flower and try to *become* its essence. The natural world will successfully make it through this transition that started in 2012 because its fundamental trait is to be harmonious.

I've noticed that my flowers are more colorful and the leaves on my trees are fuller than ever. Even though Nature sometimes seems to move slowly, I feel she, too, is being imbued with a quickened vibrational frequency. She seems to know that a swifter and more positive change will result from whatever violence this cleansing will bring.

I need to write everything down now if I want to remember it. My sense of linear logic is disappearing, and I am thinking more multidimensionally. I feel more emotional about life and less logical. My sense of fairness is permanent to me now. I can't stand to see anyone innocent get hurt. I won't go to films where animals are abused, even if I know it's only a cinematic trick.

I notice that my balance is sometimes off, which of course could be age-related, but I also see plenty of young people falling off their perches all over the place, too.

I live at eight thousand feet above sea level in Santa Fe,

New Mexico, so I know something about the effects of alti-
tude on the body. Perhaps that is why the fly population has
nearly disappeared. Maybe they went the way of the bees,
but I've noticed that insects have basically moved away from
my life. In the heat of the day (ninety-plus degrees) I can
leave my screen doors open and nothing much flies in. It's
almost as though some parts of Nature are preparing for the
Big Change.

And what is the Big Change? I go back to the shaman
who said Mother Nature is like a big mother dog shaking
off the fleas. I guess we are the fleas and whatever mess we
leave around our global house will be dealt with, one way
or another.

When I look at what is put out as entertainment today, I'm often reminded of the way the ancient Romans would stage elaborate contests and games to divert attention from the real problems of the day. Our most popular television is one form of competitive reality show or another, and the movie screens are taken up with franchised heroes and villains, nothing nuanced about their basic good-versus-evil story lines. The financial polarity is obvious. Reality TV costs very little to make, and the big screen franchises cost a fortune. What about the middle, where most of us live and, for the most part, where we choose to identify ourselves? Even the purveyors of entertainment know something big is coming, and they want to divert our attention as long as possible. "Bring on the Roman games!"

One of the most disturbing truths about show business and the effect it has on public consciousness is the development deals in place to portray extraterrestrials as evil and something to be afraid of. According to the current rules in the entertainment business, alien invasion is in the works, and that necessitates increased military protection, which is also in the works. The militarization of space will become necessary, according to the "new" entertainment. And even before that will be the manipulation of facts regarding the likelihood of asteroids crashing into big cities and wiping out the populations.

Much of the entertainment in our future seems to be developing in a way that mirrors Project Paperclip's plans to keep the military-industrial complex in charge and necessary. (General Dwight D. Eisenhower certainly knew what he was warning against when he coined that term.) It is daunting to me that scientists and military leaders of World War II devised a future for America, and maybe even the world, that involved establishing in the people a fear of:

- communism
- terrorism
- asteroids
- extraterrestrials

With Hollywood's help, it's right on schedule.

How can anyone in this world who walks upright and is

even half aware of what's really going on not search for the deeper meaning of it all? Who is in charge? Are we alone or not? How did humanity start? Why do we fight each other? Will the world come to an end? And is God out to lunch or just on a quick coffee break?

I am privileged to have had a relationship with John Mack, head of psychiatry at Harvard Medical School. Later in his career, a growing segment of his patient list consisted of people who claimed to have been taken aboard space-craft and taught the ancient history of Earth and planetary systems. The patients did not know each other, but most had been taught by the star visitors the same history as that claimed by writers and researchers such as Sitchin, Bramley, and Von Ward (more on them shortly).

Dr. Mack found himself trying to make sense of a level of psychiatry he had not been schooled in, a level of reality he had not imagined previously. He came to believe that those who had been taken aboard the crafts were telling the truth and believed what they were being taught by the star visitors.

Tragically, Dr. Mack was hit by a drunk driver and killed in London in 2004. What I found interesting was that another man named John Mack was also killed by a drunk driver that same day in London. Was it a purposeful con-spiracy? I'll never know for sure.

I miss you, John.

What if each of us could remember our untapped origins in the cosmos?

What if we didn't descend from the apes?

While Darwin's theories are widely accepted, the fact remains that there are some differences in our DNA that science has trouble explaining, and also there is the disturbing question of the missing link. What if, millions of years ago (which is only a second in cosmic time), we were visited by beings from other star systems and we were genetically engineered to become what we are now?

I have read the findings and the published works of researchers and theorists in this area of study, such as Zecharia Sitchin, William Bramley, and Paul Von Ward. I have met with them personally, asked skeptical questions of them, and now am convinced that this theory could be just as viable as—or even more viable than—any other. How could we possibly be alone in the cosmos with trillions of stars capable of supporting life? Our ancient artifacts and cave paintings, monuments and statues, as well as translated Sumerian cuneiform tablets and other ancient books, attest to long-ago visitors from the cosmos whose presence greatly influenced our planet, and our species. What if, as Sitchin, Bramley, and Von Ward all speculate, those visitors *made* us from breeding their own genetic material with a hominid species they found on Earth? Perhaps *that* is the missing link. Other scientists I have talked to say more than 20 percent of the human genome is what they call "junk DNA"— that is, DNA that is noncoding and that serves no apparent purpose. A remnant of our star ancestors? The definition of *hominid* is "one who walks upright on two legs." If the hominid were a creature of Earth, wouldn't it have been a natural candidate for such a gentle experiment? Sitchin, Bramley, and Von Ward all speculate on this theory. Sitchin and others learned the Sumerian language, which enabled them to translate the ancient cuneiform tablets. From their translations they have deduced that the star visitors were here on Earth looking for minerals, mostly gold, which they powdered down and sprayed into their skies where it served as a protective shield against toxic radiation from their own suns. The Sumerians' cuneiform tablets state in great detail that powdered gold was effective in reducing the radiation that was killing their people.

Perhaps this is why gold has always been the standard by

which we measure wealth. Gold meant *life* to a star culture, which had come close to destroying its own home world through destruction of its environment.

If the star visitors needed workers to mine the gold, why wouldn't they have used their advanced knowledge of genetic engineering to create a worker race that they would nurture and train to do the difficult work for them—hence what became a new human race over millions of years.

And what if, down through the march of time, we humans began to sense our origins while still respecting and, indeed, worshipping our star visitor creators as gods. The word for God in the Old Testament, *Eloheim,* is *plural, not singular*: *Let us make man in our own image.* So we humans have always worshipped *Gods* who are residing in the heavens. The translation from the Sumerian of one of the groups of star visitors (the Annunaki from the planet Nibiru) is "Gods who from the heaven came."

Scientists are attempting to create new humans through genetic engineering in several laboratories now. Why not first study what cosmic beings may have done millions of years ago?

I enjoy speculating on such things, since we don't have proof of where we came from anyway. We humans can't be certain who we are or what were our true origins in any definitive way, unless one chooses to believe in a literal interpretation of the Bible. And as I've said, *God (Eloheim)* is a plural word. Perhaps the Bible is correct. *Gods* created man.

What if evolution itself is speeding up?

What if the Old Testament actually contains the literal history of extraterrestrial activity on Earth?

In Genesis, we find this description of Jehovah landing on a mountaintop:

> There were thunder and lightning and a thick cloud upon the mount, and the sound of the trumpet was exceedingly loud, and all the people that were in the camp trembled.
>
> And Moses brought the people out of the camp to meet with God, and they stood at the lower part of the mountain.
>
> And Mount Sinai was altogether covered with smoke because the Lord descended upon it in fire; and the

smoke from the fire billowed upwards like the smoke of
a furnace and the whole mountain quaked greatly. (Genesis 19:16–19)

From Exodus, another description of the craft in which
Jehovah traveled:

And the Lord traveled before them by day in a pillar of
cloud, to lead them the way by night in a pillar of fire, to
give them light; to go by day and night.

He took not away the pillar of the cloud by day or the
pillar of fire by night, from in front of the people. (Exodus 13:21–22)

The Old Testament descriptions of Jehovah say no one
was permitted to approach Jehovah's mountaintop landing site except for Moses and a few select leaders. Jehovah
threatened to kill anyone else who did. People saw Jehovah
only from a distance. He usually came in a thundering craft.
Ezekiel had a more specific experience.

And I looked and behold a whirlwind came out of the
north, a great cloud and a fire flashed, causing a bright-
ness about it and out of the midst of it appeared four living creatures and this was their appearance. They had
the likeness of men.

And their feet were straight feet, and the sole of their

feet was shaped like the sole of a calf's foot, and they sparkled like burnished brass. And they had human hands under their four-sided wings. Their wings were joined together and they did not turn; when they went, they all went straight forward.

As for the appearance of their faces, they had the face of a man, and the face of a lion on the right side and the face of an ox on the left side. They also had the face of an eagle.

And when the living creatures went, the wheels went with them, and when the living creatures were lifted up from the earth, the wheels were lifted up.

And the appearance of the sky upon the heads of the living creatures was reflected as the color of the terrible crystal stretched over their heads above.

And when they went I heard the noise of their wings like the noise of great waves, as the voice of the Almighty, like the din of an army. When they stood still they lowered their wings.

And there was a voice from the crystal covering that was over their heads when they stood and had let down their wings. (Ezekiel 1:1–25)

Ezekiel describes humanlike creatures, apparently wearing metal boots and ornamented helmets. Their "wings" appeared to be retractable engines, which emitted a rumbling sound, that helped them to fly. Their heads were covered by glass or something transparent that reflected the sky above. They appeared to be in some sort of circular vehicle that had wheels. Is the book of Ezekiel the story of a person aboard a spacecraft describing the craft and the trip?

And who was Jehovah?

The name Jehovah comes from the Hebrew word *Yazeveh,* which means "he that is" or "the self-evident." Jehovah always traveled through the sky in what seemed to be a smoky aircraft, always a moving object.

Was Jehovah an astronaut who wanted the people of Earth to believe he was God?

What if Jesus was an astronaut?

What if these "Eloheim," these visitors from the stars, were regarded as gods and creators by those who wrote the Old Testament? What if these gods abused their power and demanded worship? What if they demanded the divine right of kings? What if their power became absolute—Jehovah, Yahweh, Horus, Isis, etc.—and all humans were expected to become subservient to their will and power?

What if the result of the cross-breeding of star visitors and hominids became a new order of religious leaders? The Eloheim said, "Let's make man in *our* own image." The word was *our,* which is plural. What if that offspring, resonating with the DNA of the all-powerful creators, later saw themselves as the kings and queens of new religions, until human beings found themselves chafing under the edicts of ancient illuminated ones who claimed to be ruling in the name of God in Heaven with the divine right of kings . . . those who from the Heavens came to Earth in chariots that belched fire and spoke in commanding tongues. "When the sons of Gods found the daughters of men fair" (Genesis 6:2), a new race was born: the new humans who have the DNA of the *gods* within themselves.

What if Adam and Eve were told not to eat the fruit from the tree of knowledge as a control mechanism? What if the "snake" was an ET *protector* who was trying to tell them to be curious about the world and their place in it, because they had a right to know. In ancient times, snakes were used to represent wise people who had the ability to heal. That is why the caduceus, the symbol of the medical profession, includes two snakes.

What if the snake was not the deceiver, but was instead the conduit to spiritual and healing knowledge? Maybe religious propaganda after the fact turned him into the heavy. What if the snake wanted Adam and Eve to grow in knowledge because he knew they were being taken advantage of by another ET? What if the shame of nakedness was not about the body but more about their new understanding that they were considered less than complete? Did the Eloheim want the new human servants kept in the dark about their own spiritual power on purpose?

What if the Eloheim "creators" purposely addicted

mankind to the physical body to divert attention from our spiritual power? Was that why Adam and Eve were told not to eat the fruit of the tree of knowledge or the tree of life? Did the Eloheim "creators" punish Adam and Eve for being too curious about life and spirit by condemning them to live in a land east of Eden, where they would toil for their food?

> Cursed is the ground for you, in toil will you eat its yield for all the days of your life. Thorns, too, and thistles will it bring forth to you, as you eat the plants from the field.
>
> By the sweat of your face will you eat bread, until you return to the ground, for out of it you were taken, for dust you are and to dust you will return. (Genesis 3:17–19)

Doesn't this read like a rather insensitive and cruel Eloheim and an interesting description of human and perhaps extraterrestrial genetic engineering?

What if curiosity were the original sin?

Did the Eloheim "creators" intend for mankind to live our entire lives regarding only a material physical existence? This would leave humans precious little time to pursue the art and science of the spirit of our true nature. Were we not to be allowed knowledge of our own spirit? Were we instead educated to worship only them as gods of all Knowledge and Wisdom, because we were intended to remain as

servants of the gods to do their will and not know the power
of our own free spirit?

"Thou shalt not eat of the fruit of the tree of knowledge
of good and evil."

What if the long-ago Eloheim gods became alarmed that
their new servants were now united and wanted to build a
rocket starship as their masters had done? Was that crude
ship the Tower of Babel? What if the servant race all spoke
one language, which was instrumental in maintaining their
cooperative unity?

> And they said, come, let us build ourselves a city and
> a tower whose top will reach the skies, and let us make
> a name for ourselves, otherwise we will be scattered all
> over the face of the Earth.

> And the Lord Gods came down to see the city and
> the tower, which the men servants were building and the
> Lord Gods said, "Look, the people are united and they
> have all one language and this they begin to do and now
> nothing will stop them from doing what they take in
> their minds to do. Let us go down and there confuse
> their language so that they cannot understand one an-
> other's speech."

> So the Lord Gods scattered them abroad from there all
> over the face of the Earth and they stopped building the
> city and the tower.

> Therefore the name of it is called Babel, because the

Lord Gods did there confuse the language of the entire Earth and from there did the Lord Gods scatter them abroad over the face of the Earth. (Genesis 11:7–9)

There are ancient stories and legends all over the earth that support the Tower of Babel event, because the "servants" were scattered, and each group developed a new language of its own. The Japanese, the Alaskan Inuit, the native peoples of South America, the Egyptians—they all have traditions stating that their earliest forefathers had either been transported by human-like "gods" to where the modern descendants live today or that these "gods" had been the source of the local languages or writing. And from then on, when trying to understand each other, the languages became "Babel."

Were those acts by the Lord "gods" the first examples of a divide-and-conquer technique that would keep the human race from reaching its true spiritual potential?

Are the answers to all these "who are we?" questions truly and literally to be found in the bestselling book of all time, the Holy Bible?

I wonder what went into the DNA recipe of genetic engineering that we still suffer from. Is the attraction to suffering, conflict, and pain built into our DNA so that we can never grow out of our dependence on the gods that made us? Are *they* the missing link?

What if this theory is the basic truth? And it's right there in the pages of the Bible! What if not only are we not alone, but we are in fact the descendants of the star beings? We are doing the same thing today, but without knowledge as advanced as those who traveled millions of cosmic miles to get here. This theory does not impugn the existence of God. In fact, it enhances it.

What if those people who claim to have been abducted by aliens are telling the truth and they have learned vitally important information that we need to know?

In the exchanges I have had with people who have been educated aboard spacecrafts (abductees and contactees), they claim that most ET civilizations are also searching for the meaning of the creator God. Others don't believe in a god or gods at all; they opt for happenstance creating life in the universe. One ET civilization believes that God is a giant mathematical computer, and they say they can prove it. The diversity of opinions and viewpoints is a great entertainment for me. I find the simplest explanations make the most sense. Rather like a movie, really.

Even as I put these speculations about our origins into

words, I can see the eye-rolling and hear people tossing this book down and throwing their arms up into the air. But what if all this is hiding in plain sight in the Bible and only subject to interpretation? And what else is there to *wonder* about that is more deeply entertaining? Why should anyone be upset at such speculation? *No one* knows the answer, and no faith, if it's strong enough, is besmirched by another person's ideas or speculations. But . . .

If what I ruminate upon is even partially true, doesn't that mean we humans are only an infinitesimal part of a gigantic cosmic puzzle? Are other cosmic beings watching us? The ancient translations continually speak of the "watchers from the heavens." Are they influencing us? Or, as I've been told, are they forbidden to interfere with the affairs of the earth's human race? And are each of the five races on earth simply descendants corresponding to populations in the cosmos?

Most of the information that I've found comes from human beings who have been taken aboard the spacecrafts and put through a crash course in things the star beings want us to know. For example:

There are extraterrestrials who have a genetic base similar to humans of Earth. They appear to be of normal height (five foot six) and tend to be fair-skinned with blond hair. Many "contactees" claim they were abducted by those from the Orion constellation, or what are called the Greys, and have been trained by the Greys as servants.

There are other extraterrestrials who are also fair-skinned

and blond who are genuinely highly evolved spiritually and are benevolent in every way. These are the Pleiadians and they feel a kinship toward humans and are the only aliens thus far who can be completely trusted by Earth humans at this time. Some contactees have said these extraterrestrials offered to be of service to humanity but were rebuffed. As a result, they have taken a "hands off" approach to the human race for the time being. They say their forefathers are our forefathers. The Bible talks of the "sweet influence of the Pleiades."

The Greys (short, with gray skin, deep holes for eyes, and a round O for a mouth) come from Zeta Reticulum, the fourth planet out from $Zeta^2$ Reticuli, near Barnard's Star, which is a neighboring star system in the Orion constellation. The Orion star system is a fairly small collection of faint stars, of which Zeta is hardly visible to the naked eye, even though it is relatively close to us, at approximately forty light-years. The dim point of light known to us as Zeta Reticuli is actually a binary star system and its two stars, Zeta Reticuli and $Zeta^2$ Reticuli, are each very much like our own yellow sun. It is not visible in our Northern Hemisphere.

Orion Greys are from a star system near the shoulder Orion called Bellatrix. These are the shortest of the group (about 3.5 feet tall). The Bellatrix Greys and the Zeta Reticuli Greys are related genetically and look very much alike except for size. The Bible speaks of the "bonds of Orion."

The reptilian races are said to come from Alpha Draconia, Epsilon Bootïs, and Rigel. The amphibian types come from Larga. Lyra was a multirace and multicultural system that was the origin of many races. Its inhabitants destroyed their own home world through nuclear wars, and with the demise of their system, their segregated groups went to various other planets, some of which had to be "engineered" to support life.

I repeat, our Bible makes reference to Orion, Pleiades, and Arcturus with statements describing their cultures. "The bonds of Orion," the "sweet influence of the Pleiades," and the location of Arcturus.

The star people teach that acceptance and understanding of reincarnation negate the existence of evil because the laws of cause and effect explain negative occurrences. What one puts out in one lifetime is returned in another—karma, in other words, not some evil outside force or power.

Some star systems have a different understanding of evolution than we have on Earth. Because of this, they can continually improve their conditions. Because they know they are bound by the laws of cause and effect, they each take responsibility for their own actions, for what we call "evil." Every action has a reaction, whether it occurs in the present lifetime or later.

This karmic law, the star visitors claim, was lost on Earth long ago. Therefore we are troubled by the "demonic" element of human dualism, from which there is no escape, and for which there is no explanation. In other words, we believe the Devil (Lucifer) exists inside and outside of us, allowing us to completely abdicate responsibility for our own karmic actions.

Some of the star visitors also teach that every unselfish deed, every act of self-sacrifice, heightens an individual's feeling of personal value and satisfaction. Therefore, people are more at peace with themselves and enjoy a happier state. The visitors say there is no alternative; only a race with a high level of unselfishness or, as they call it, "an immaterial structure," can survive. When a people are free of material influence, their unselfish mental attitude allows them to raise free and happy children.

The star people also say, "We must teach children to be expressive with their feelings. They will become eloquent in order to put their feelings into words." They will be characterized by honesty, spontaneity, and enthusiasm. Their helpfulness to others will raise their loving relationships above the physical to great spiritual heights. The star people say they seek adventure in the quantity and depths of their human contacts, and find it a pity that they can embrace only one human at a time.

There is so much to speculate upon. For years I have felt like a newly aware teenager armed with just enough clandestine information to tease me into being obsessed with learning more of the most fundamental truths of life itself, while suspecting also that a giant cover-up is in play because we humans are not equipped to process it. To quote Jack Nicholson

in the film *A Few Good Men*, "You can't handle the truth."
And as my boundaries broaden, I ask myself: Is military intelligence behind the cover-up of the "Gods in sky boats"? Is the
all-powerful military putting its force and taxpayer financing
behind covering up what could easily be the most entertaining science fiction movie and video game in human history?

The general population would probably love to see and
know what military intelligence knows. Sharing their information would make a lot of money for the Pentagon and
finance whatever new wars they want to wage in order to
justify their existence. Imagine paying the military for entertaining information as to who we really are. Yes, that's a
good one for Hollywood—easy-to-find financing and distribution. Maybe the military should act as technical advis-
ers so as to prepare the public for a cosmic landing and a
Close Encounter.

Since everything is timing, as they tell us, the publicity
and marketing machines are in place for an easy sell, since
millions of humans thought the world would begin its end
after 2012. The public might believe the movie with real extraterrestrials, because we all know we could use some help.
The military would get off the hook for a master cover-up
in a democracy, the Church would stay as it is, the believers
would not be made to feel sacrilegious, and people would
finally get it straight that life is show business anyway. I say,
entertain the people into understanding the truth. They can
handle that, and the conspiracy theorists win, too.

We'd have a first, second, and third act, which is a necessary structure for good entertainment. First act: ETs came to Earth. Second act: ETs bred with what they found walking upright and produced a new race. Third act: New race nearly destroys itself. ETs watch and don't like what they see. They reveal themselves and scold their Earth-bound descendants and start anew. God stays in heaven, looking down with a benevolent smile at his "gods" and his gods' children. No problem. Then military intelligence can come out of hiding; the Church is not jeopardized, because it welcomed brothers and sisters from space under God anyway. Science can say "even God is a scientist," and Mother Nature will finally get a breather.

This is my idea of an entertaining "intelligent design" or "theory of evolution."

What if "let there be light" was a reference to human beings witnessing the brilliant lighting up of a star craft?

What if the karmic dramas we've experienced over the last twenty-six thousand years had come to an end on December 21, 2012, the date described (ad nauseam) as the "end" of the Mayan calendar? But what if the Mayan calendar is a calendar of consciousness, and its end marks the start of a shift in our human consciousness? Could it have happened and we just do not know it yet?

The end of the twenty-six-thousand-year period is also the end of the precession of the equinoxes. Each of us was born under a cosmic sign that carries behavior and consciousness patterns for that lifetime. Perhaps we choose which sign to be born under according to what we need to learn, and there are karmic returns and paybacks from lifetime to lifetime according to our past behavior. But when the time period came to an end on December 21, 2012—which was the end of the precession of these cosmic signs—perhaps the karmic laws of cause and effect came to an end, too, and with new consciousness, we will now be able to start all over without having to drag the drama of the past around with us. I often think about what that would mean for humanity and our home planet.

Is that why the Mayan calendar and other ancient texts and drawings couldn't see anything beyond 2012? Was karma the "beast" referred to in Revelations? When the beast was destroyed, there would be a thousand years of peace. Does that mean we will have a thousand years finally to get it right, and then we go for the next twenty-five thousand years?

Perhaps karma consciousness is basically the buildup of the returning energy to its source. We have all lived so many lifetimes filled with suffering and tragedy. Perhaps we have experienced being part of civilizations that have risen and fallen over millions of years, and the fear we felt during those experiences remains in our soul memory. What if we are all products of the memory of what has gone before, and our trust in the future is at a low ebb now? The demise of enough civilizations could almost make us addicted to failure, prejudiced against our own success because it has never seemed to last.

If the karma of it all ceases and desists, perhaps we will be "resurrected" from fear. Without fear we could have long-lasting peace in our souls. Without ancient karmic memories, perhaps we will be "home again" as children of the Light and will understand that we can trust love, or, more importantly, we can trust *trust*.

Perhaps this is why people seemed so willing to believe that 2012 denoted doom and gloom. Perhaps we were addicted to this belief because it had happened too many times. Even hope is defined in relation to its alternative, disaster. The etymological definition of the word *disaster* is *dis* (torn asunder) *aster* (from the astral [stars]). I believe we have been torn away from the original divinity of the stars.

Perhaps the cessation of the karma of the last twenty-six thousand years will enable us to begin again without fear. History will definitely need a new script, and all of us— humans and star beings, extraterrestrial actors—will have a chance to play our parts a different way. The question is, *Will the audience like it?*

What if the body is merely a vehicle for souls to act out their parts, lifetime after lifetime, until they finally get it right? Is each life an audition for the Big Director in the Sky, everyone choosing the part he or she has come in to play?

What if it's true that we each choose what we need to learn each time around, and we choose the people whom our souls have actually had past experiences with?

What if we really choose our mothers and fathers and family members from a cast of soul characters we know will afford us the opportunity to learn what we most need to learn? And what if we cast ourselves alongside characters we dislike? Maybe it's just another way of learning—the hard way.

What if suffering is the way we choose to learn compassion? If we don't experience something ourselves, how can we understand what someone else is going through?

What if raising one's consciousness is really about upgrading the Divine in ourselves?

What if anger and rage are leftover karmic experiences we haven't processed, balanced, and cleared up?

The residue of each karmic experience, either in this lifetime or others that went before, still resides in our soul's memory. We remember the terrifying emotional circumstances that preceded our life today, and we haven't calibrated the reasons for those experiences. We have lived in many civilizations and have cried through many periods of destruction. Fear is only a part of our soul memory, a part that breeds anger and hostility and rage at us and anyone around us.

What if fear is the predominant human emotion because of our dimly remembered past life experiences? Fear will remain our primary motivation in everything we do until we come to the realization that fear is only what we think it is. Since the soul never dies, what is there to fear regarding death?

I don't see Nature fearing anything. She is just in need of cleansing.

I am told that nuclear war is nothing to fear because that is one human activity that our star neighbors will not allow to happen. Stopping a nuclear war would not be considered karmic interference because a nuclear war would jeopardize their safety and happiness in the cosmos as well. I have been told that nuclear explosions "melt" the human soul, and it will not be tolerated.

The human powers told us after Hiroshima and Nagasaki that fear of nuclear war would keep the world at peace. But I believe that fear has a boiling point. And when we reach the level of "no fear of fear," we lose our sanity. Would the star crafts come out of the lakes and oceans to stop us? Nature would sing then.

What if God purposefully doesn't interfere with anything we do?

What if we learned that there is no such thing as a victim?

What if we learned that most of the people who are murdered willingly choose to go that way in order to balance their karma? In other words, on a superconscious level they understand that they were murderers in a previous incarnation. Since all energy returns to its source, it is necessary to experience that which we put out. It is, science says, a law of physics. No energy ever dies. It simply changes form and returns to its source.

What if all the horror on the earth is basically karma balancing?

What if most of the Holocaust victims were balancing their karma from ages before, when they were Roman soldiers putting Christians to death, the Crusaders who murdered millions in the name of Christianity, soldiers with Hannibal, or those who stormed across the Near East with Alexander? The energy of killing is endless and will be experienced by the kill*er* and the kill*ee*.

When I was in Brazil studying psychic healers, I asked them how they explained their extraordinary results. In psychic healing, surgery is performed without the use of instruments or the making of any incision. The healer's hands enter the body and perform necessary procedures on internal organs, then are removed without any harm to the patient. I saw people have their hearts removed and repaired, their eyes taken out and cleaned, cripples who were made able to walk again, and so much more. I *saw* these things that confused my Western, left-brained sense of reality. The healers explained that the body is really nothing but "coagulated thought," an illusion that by consensus we agreed was, and decreed to be, "physical." The ancients understood this and regarded the physical world as the forms taken by thoughts, and thus were able to heal through thought. For psychic healers, repairing the body is an exercise in spiritual rebalancing.

When I probed into why they were healers, most of them said it wasn't they who were doing the healing anyway. They said human souls that had previously committed egregiously violent acts on other humans in past lives desperately wanted to balance their karma. So these souls channeled their psychic healing energies through these pres-ent-day healers.

A few of the psychic healers told me that their "channeled doctors" had been Nazis in the concentration camps who had been horribly cruel in their treatment of the prisoners. They desired to balance their cruelty now with healing.

The psychics said killing of any kind is the highest cosmic crime because it robs the killee of his or her learning experience, and the purpose of life is to learn love and to grasp the connection of the Creator to all creation. In effect, we are all One.

In being open channels to the healing energy of these repentant souls, they said they'd come to see that the definition of Evil is imposing one's will on another. We all get to choose the way we want to bring balance to ourselves, and in doing so hopefully we learn from our previous existences.

If "an eye for an eye, a tooth for a tooth" is another definition of karma and not just an ancient form of justice, then that which we put out in one lifetime is returned in a subsequent lifetime. Because science says, "All energy returns to its source," is this another example of science and spirituality coming together?

What if we could see real-life "dailies" like we do in "reel" life?

Imagine if we each had a personalized movie screen on which we could play back scenes of our behavior—the good, the bad, and the downright ugly? We could study the screen for clues regarding our real-life behavior. We could critique our wardrobe, our hair, our dialogue, and, most important, our actions and their repercussions. Maybe we could see why we cast other people in certain roles in our lives.

Let's extend this idea: What if the life behavior screen were capable of showing us scenes from whatever past lives we wanted to view? Imagine what it would mean to see, on the screen, the past lives we had with the people who give us the most heartache today. We could possibly see their motivation and point of view. Out of the past we'd begin to understand the present. As the old saying goes, those who ignore the lessons of the past are condemned to repeat them. A past life behavior screen might give us some insight into the inexplicable behavior of Hitler, Pol Pot, Hannibal, Henry VIII, Dick Cheney, etc. I'd also like to see the past life screen of Jesus, or Gandhi, or Abraham Lincoln. What possessed these people to act as they did in the lifetimes we can identify?

When I was in Peru shooting *Out on a Limb*, I met a teacher whose amazing personal story started me thinking along these lines. He'd been an intellectual skeptic before he was taken aboard a spacecraft. He had spent his life in a small town of twenty-five thousand people. He said the occupants of the craft wanted to warn him of an impending disaster in his village. They pointed to a screen and ushered him to sit down in front of it. They turned it on, and he saw himself as a young boy. He said he remembered doing some of the things he saw on the screen; others, he'd forgotten all about. It was as though a camera had followed him around. His life unfolded on the screen: his teenage years, the people he knew, his marriage, his children, the death of his wife. When he asked how such a thing was possible, the space people told him that no energy is ever lost, and that includes experience and knowledge. It is stored in what is known as the akashic records, they said. They indicated that a kind of "advanced spiritual technology" makes it possible to bring past energy into form so that it seems reenacted—something like a movie of life. My friend in Peru told me that he felt like he'd had a lesson in the *technology of the spirit*, its component parts, its history, its sophisticated state of consciousness.

The star people then let my teacher friend understand why they were showing him the film. The screen shifted to a long-range exterior shot of his town. As he watched, the ground began to shake, until finally a volcano erupted. Lava and a mountain waterfall merged together and roared ferociously into the town. Buildings quaked and collapsed. The town was deluged in lava and water. The screen showed a news report saying that nineteen thousand people had died in the disaster.

My friend was devastated by what he saw on the screen and asked why he was being shown such an event. The space people told him to warn the residents of the town. What he saw was a future event whose impact could be mitigated if he warned them in time.

He left the craft and the next day proceeded to do exactly what they had suggested. Some people heeded his warning and evacuated; the majority didn't. Not long after, news reports showed horrific footage that was nearly identical to what my friend had seen on the screen in the craft.

When we discussed all this, he said he had learned that all time happens concurrently, but that we are afforded certain free-will choices if we can discern the "consciousness of the Future." He said that the most advanced science of consciousness was what we call God, the creator. He said the cosmos itself was made up of self-aware consciousness. He said the space people told him that they were studying what that God consciousness was, just as we human Earth people were. They were just a few hundred thousand years ahead of us.

He said they want to be of help to us, but there is so much we don't want to know. He said the visitors had been rebuffed in their desire to help so many times in the past by Earth's rulers that there were now trust issues involved. How could they feel confident in dealing with a race of people who willfully conducted their affairs according to what they did *not* want to know? It seemed to the star visitors that secrets and fear were the predominant values of our planet's inhabitants. And so our fate is up to us. However, suggestions from those who have seen and experienced more than we have are available if we'd care to listen.

The star visitors said that every human being could benefit from viewing his or her own life-history movie. We'd catch up on our true identity. And if we were deeply curious, they could show us the history of our various lives down through time. That's the Show Business of "akashic karma," proving that nothing ever dies.

What if we could experience psychic liberation?

What if the Earth is moving into a higher dimension? sion?

Quantum scientists are saying that this third-dimension Earth is bypassing the fourth-dimensional frequency and moving into the fifth-dimensional frequency. As I understand it, that means everything will be moving faster. Thoughts, events, emotions, improvements, complications—all manner of life will move at a faster rate. We speak about how fast the pace of life is now, but what does that really mean? Does it mean our consciousness is speeding up? I notice everyone thinking faster, speaking faster, becoming impatient and full of rage faster. Many people (including the young and middle-aged) tell me they feel increasingly prone to a sense of disorientation.

For example, they'll climb into their car and it will somehow feel unfamiliar, as though they've never been in it before. When they are driving, it feels as though the car is not obeying the brake, or the controls are different. Sometimes they go to familiar places and don't recognize any of the usual landmarks at all. Suddenly, they feel lost and unfamiliar. It's as though they've been transported to some distant place. They calm themselves, and then it's familiar again. Whatever episode like this they describe to me, I can identify with it. It's happening to me, too. Is this a case of aging faster?

I'll walk into a room with an intended purpose and immediately forget why I'm there. Or I'll look for something, and even though it's right in front of me, I can't see it. I know it's there, but I can't see it.

Frequently traveled highways and streets seem unfamiliar but somehow remind me of the past. I'm prone to forgetting important personal events that I was present for and a part of. My closest friends seem to be a conglomeration of other people. I see other identities in them. They see the same in me.

When I observe people laughing and joking around, I find myself wondering how they can be so frivolous. I am particularly perturbed by all the chirpy perkiness so prevalent on news shows when the anchors and reporters try to outdo each other being funny, even while reporting on some awful disaster. And yet . . . when I see people legitimately depressed and morose, I want to smack them for their defeatist attitude.

Many people tell me they want to spend more time alone with their thoughts and feelings. Or even better, alone with their dogs and cats—they've recognized how much more balanced animals seem to be than humans.

When I hear that members of the president's Secret Service detail are boffing prostitutes in Colombia and then resigning because of extramarital affairs, I wonder if people anywhere still have a work ethic. The workmen who do odd jobs in my home never seem to bring the right equipment and have to make several trips in order to accomplish whatever it is they were hired to do. Workers on my roof left a water valve open that precipitated the flooding of my bedroom. The water ran down my bookcases and tables and chairs and soaked into the carpet. I found myself treading ankle deep in water as I tried to figure out not only why it had happened, but why I had the feeling that I was walking in a dream. When I confronted them, the workers didn't blink. I guess it wasn't happening in *their* dream!

Dreamlike is the descriptive term I'd use these days for life—I'm in a movable dream, as if I'm living proof that what we think of as reality is only an illusion. If that is so, then why get emotional or judgmental about anything? I value my work ethic because I feel it keeps me sane. I value my sanity because I feel it will come in handy when the shift occurs. My new motto: Shift Happens.

What if we changed the way we celebrate birthdays?

I think the stress reduction would be enormous. Why? Because a birthday celebration is a record keeper, not only of years but of values and loves and hates. You remember the promises you made to yourself and never fulfilled. You remember whom you disappointed and who disappointed you. You recognize how the present is different from the idea you once had of your future happiness.

Every minute of your birthday, you are self-conscious about who you are and who you're not and who you should be celebrating with. If you're a spiritually oriented person, as I like to think I am, you might try to indulge in the discipline of projecting what you and the universe can co-create during the next year. For example, I know I should acknowledge the talent and power "God" gave me and pay it deeper respect. I try to analyze what "God" is and what I'm really here for and whether I've lived up to my potential.

When the birthday phone calls come, I want to talk to everyone, but the truth is I know I'm giving them short shrift with my time. Why? Because someone else is calling and I want to be polite to everybody.

The birthday flowers come, and my concern, more than my appreciation, is making sure I know who sent what. I really want to be alone with big birthday thoughts, but I must acknowledge those in my life whom I care about and who care about me. I worry that people will spend too much money for a birthday gift because they think I'm used to the best. I tell them "no gifts," but they send them anyway.

I used to wonder if the reason I don't like opening gifts is because I place little value on myself. But I know that's not true. In fact, I'd say the opposite. What I'm really concerned about is whether the money the gift giver spent is hard on their budget. Therefore, I don't like gifts. No one knows what to get me anyway. I've never gotten a really expensive gift—like a car, or a diamond bracelet, or a trip somewhere. None of my lovers, my ex-husband, or my close friends could afford such things anyway. Money has so much to do with how I and others celebrate birthdays that I don't like thinking about it.

I have celebrated my birthday in many foreign locations where I told no one about the occasion. It was a little lonely, but it allowed me to avoid all the things I don't like about people knowing. I've been thrown one or two attempted "surprise" birthday parties, but somehow I always knew beforehand it was happening.

My seventy-fifth birthday was nice. I gave myself a party and insisted on several people coming. That was easier for everyone because of the certainty involved—no ambiguity. As I grow older, I've noticed my birthdays becoming more of a celebration of longevity. That's nice.

The one thing I do regardless of where I am is take time to project what I want to happen in the next year. My birthday projections usually come to pass because I own the moment I was born, and with that ownership I feel certain I can co-create what I want for the coming twelve months. Here's how it works: I imagine what I want to happen. I picture it three times—one for mind, one for body, and one for spirit. I send the pictures out into the universe and let them go. Then I write each projection down three times—one for mind, one for body, and one for spirit. I put the paper away and don't look at it until my next birthday. Most of the time everything I projected comes true.

Birthdays are for utilizing your power to make your own life better—and the world a better place. One thing I know for sure: we all possess the power to make the pictures in our minds become the "reality" in which we live.

What if we could celebrate all the birthdays we ever had? And by that I mean including the birthdays that happened a few hundred thousand years ago. What would the human race be like if seven billion of us remembered how many times we've been around and what we learned or didn't learn about ourselves each time? What if we realized that most of the people in our lives today are souls we have known, and have learned from and with, over and over?

What if we admitted that we have all been male, female, transgender, gay, straight, and androgynous at one time or another? In fact, what if we understood that choosing a gender was no different than choosing an outfit to wear, and that the chosen physical appearance was accompanied by behavioral tendencies that matched?

What if we remembered having been slaughtered in a war and could live up to the learning that we never want that to happen to us or anyone else again? From that day on, there would be no more war.

What if we remembered ruining one of our lives out of jealousy or greed, and realized that the tendency toward those same emotions was still present in this lifetime? If we remembered, perhaps we would deal with such destructive feelings more sanely and constructively this time.

What if we understood that death doesn't happen, because nothing ever dies, it just changes form? Perhaps if we understood there was no such thing as death, we would stop killing each other!

What if our birthdays were celebrated as an in-depth review of what we've accomplished and not accomplished for all the centuries up to now, and from that we got suggestions of what to work on in the following year?

Such a review would give our lives purpose and intentionality. We would be more in touch with who we are, who we're not, and who we want to be.

The question then is: What is the source of a review like this? Is it God? Is it our own higher self? And is there any difference between the two?

What if our souls have simply forgotten how many incarnations they have had?

What if we had total recall of our lives on other worlds?

What if I, for some reason, couldn't be creative and work?

With advancing years, I think about this more and more. I do believe that wisdom is the reward of aging. What I do in films, on stage, and on paper doesn't take a lot of physical activity. My mind is more active than ever with creative, imaginative ideas (some of which could even be true), and I don't suffer too much over what people will think.

I am more than happy with my life, and glad I dodged another marriage bullet (my husband passed away twenty-five years ago). I live in beautiful, comfortable surroundings that are paid for, and I don't eat much. I enjoy sharing what I care about and what interests me, but frankly, I'm not sure I care about whether anyone hears me or not.

I write what I'm thinking because I enjoy it. I'll help publicize, but I don't watch grosses. The same goes for films. I play a part in a little movie because I like it. I've been through the "it's not good for your career" years. I don't care whether something is a hit or not. Again, I'll help publicize it, but I have to enjoy that, too, or I don't show up or stay. If there's dark chocolate with nuts involved, I'll stay longer.

I care about my health but get discouraged over my expanding waistline, mostly because it entails buying new clothes. I don't like to shop for anything. Most of what I need I get from brochures. I don't know how to buy online and I don't like giving out my credit card number to a computer. My overhead is not high, so I don't really need to go to work. But the thought of not being creative and expressing myself is rather paralyzing for me. The "what if" part of my personality is essential to my life force. Sometimes I think that speculation is more fun than knowledge. I just turn the answers into more questions anyway.

I have not learned to leave my body voluntarily. Astral projection sometimes scares me. Out-of-body experiences are rare for me, and I like them to happen when I'm sleeping. It's the ultimate in "letting go." Letting go is the key to happiness for me as I grow older.

I don't like feeling nervous, so I trust in whatever guides and angels I have and let them handle whatever might be concerning me. One day when I was hiking and feeling nervous, something told me to look down. I did, and there was a flat, bluish stone on which was written TRUST. I sleep with it beside my bed every night.

I don't like to party anymore. I've had enough of that. I like having dinner with a few friends. I drive myself everywhere, but don't like driving at night. So I have an early dinner somewhere with friends while it's still light. And I can find better parking spaces earlier, too.

People ask me what the most difficult part of aging is. I find myself describing new choreography for getting out of the bathtub! I installed a hot tub on my porch, which I can be warm in while I'm gazing at the stars, wondering who and what they are.

I hike with Terry and Buddy-Bub every morning, but I'm noticing that the hikes are getting shorter and over flatter terrain.

I'm not a person who tolerates being sick. I have no real awareness that I'm actually going to be eighty years old soon. It's an affront to me, because I think I'm still young.

I lounge on my deck in the breeze and sun, with Terry and Buddy-Bub sitting proudly next to me like two Egyptian Anubises. The breeze sings, the hills echo with the calls of birds, a coyote howls to the daylight moon, and I say to myself, "How could it be any better?"

Then I get up quickly and I find out!

What if enlightenment is inevitable?

What if the Director never says, "Cut"?

What if this isn't . . . The End?